T0208697

This Isn't Real, Is It?

REBECCA VILJOEN

WESTBOW
PRESS®
A DIVISION OF THOMAS NELSON
& ZONDERVAN

WestBow Press books may be ordered through booksellers or by contacting:

WestBow Press
A Division of Thomas Nelson & Zondervan
1663 Liberty Drive
Bloomington, IN 47403
www.westbowpress.com
1 (866) 928-1240

ISBN: 978-1-9736-4896-3 (sc)
ISBN: 978-1-9736-4897-0 (e)

Print information available on the last page.

WestBow Press rev. date: 01/09/2019

Contents

Prologue

Just about everyone has an unexplained, miraculous, unusual or just plain hilarious incident to recount. It is usually something that is unique, or happens very seldom. Some people are accident prone.

My brother was such a one. He was prone to such things as having a poisonous spider run up his plank, in woodworking class, and bite him (a happening which caused such consternation and excitement that it was the subject of a newspaper report). He also set himself alight smoking, while cleaning his bicycle with petrol.

My mother had a few unusual amusing stories. Once she went to the restroom before going in to see a film. She placed her tickets on top of the cistern. When she flushed the toilet, there was such a violent and enthusiastic water rush that an updraft was created. The tickets were blown into the air and, before my bemused mother could react, sucked down the U-bend with no hope of retrieval. The manager of the cinema was so entertained by her complaint that he replaced the lost tickets, with tickets for more expensive seats.

I am prone to a variety of incidents – more than my fair share. I say incidents because I am seldom injured, even though some of the incidents involve falls. At times, things happen, everyday. Sometimes, more than one thing happens during a day. I began to wonder if I was causing them, but some of them were so beyond anything I could imagine, I am now convinced there is a factor I do not control.

I used to phone my dad and stepmother from time to time, when they lived in a different city, and tell them about recent happenings. Then, they came to live with us.

I was passing the door to their sitting room one day, after they had been with us for some time, and overheard May (my stepmother) talking to her visitor.

"You know things happen to that girl. Every day! I thought she was making them up . . . (my mouth fell open in horror) but a year in this house and I would believe anything!"

Making them up! I was shocked. For what possible reason would I make them up?!

May came to enjoy hearing about the things which happened to me. I made her laugh often. She came off blood pressure tablets, after a year under our roof.

My dad and May have since passed on, and I miss telling them my stories. I especially miss watching May hiss with laughter until her head was in her lap.

May suggested I write down the things which happened each day in a diary, and at the end of a year I would have a book. She even gave me the diary to write in. I did write down a few things, but I ran out of time. I was too busy experiencing more incidents.

I am, finally, getting round to making a concerted effort. This is a collection of true incidents, which I absolutely swear I did not make up, or even exaggerate. It has come to my notice that, May was not the only person to think I was making them up. The guardian angel, with the inventive and wacky sense of humor, that I hold responsible for what happens to me, has recently been kind enough to arrange witnesses for the last couple of things which occurred.

The stories appear to have a type of healing and cheering power, for many people. They certainly, make me feel better when things are getting overwhelming. That is why I thought I would share them.

Six other books along similar lines are to follow shortly. (*Living in Africa, Animal People, The Birthday of My Brain* (about being a teacher), *The Slow Burner* (about marriage), *Travels with Others* and *Mice on Toast* (from birth to marriage). There are other books I have on my mind, but those listed, are the ones which have been started, and are in various stages of completion.

To protect people's identities, names (including mine) have been changed and the events are not in chronological order.

My thanks go to my good friends and May, who were entertained and encouraged me to write these experiences down.

Dedicated to my beloved stepmother,who loved to laugh.

Meeting May

Considering what happened the first few times I met May, I really think she should have realised I was not making things up.

My father, Louis, brought May around about 5pm one evening. We had met her once – at our wedding. It was a surprise visit. When they arrived I was in the bathroom with my two young sons.

I came to greet the visitors, and we went into the lounge to chat. After a while, I caught a movement out the side of my eye. When I turned my head, I saw a stream of water flowing past the lounge door and out of the front door.

In the excitement of meeting May, I had forgotten about the boys' bath water. The bath had overflowed and having filled the bathroom, had made its way into the passage, travelled down the length, turned the corner into the hall, and continued out of the front door.

Dad and May had to leave by the back door.

I had to go next door to ask my neighbour for newspapers, take all the passage carpet up and mop for hours, before laying newspaper down.

My next encounter with May was when she and my dad were invited to dinner. May was diabetic. I had planned a simple, nutritious (and

I hoped – delicious) meal. Sautéed potatoes were on the menu – just a few on her plate.

After pouring oil into a pot, I began heating it. To my confusion, a thick brown substance formed in the pot after a while. I emptied out the oil and started again, but the same thing happened. I smelt the oil – it smelt fine. I was in a hurry and did not have any other oil, so I decided to carry on. The potatoes were sautéed – they looked fine and smelt fine. Everything looked good and colourful on the plates, but when we tasted the potatoes – they were sweet!

Then I put two and two together. My husband, Ted, had helped me clean up a few days previously, after I had been making koeksisters. Part of the process involves a thin syrup. Ted had mistaken the syrup for oil and poured it into the oil bottle.

Good start to our relationship – I feed a diabetic stepmother potatoes cooked in syrup!

Our next meeting took place at their house in Mutare. The only incident was that I broke the pull switch in the bathroom. That seemed to be a weakness of mine. I had done the same thing to the pull switch in my mother-in-law's bathroom and in and the bathroom and kitchen, in the flatlet I lived in before marriage.

We got away without farther incident but had to return after we had gone about a hundred kilometers on our way home, because I had left my handbag.

A few months later May was coming for tea at our house. I was determined that nothing untoward was going to happen that time. I planned everything carefully.

Unfortunately, the car had to go in for a service the day they were in town. It meant more organisation, but I was confident that everything would go well. I arranged for a friend to pick me up and take me home from the garage. I left plenty of time to make some cheese scones and lay the tea things out after I got back.

Everything went according to plan. I dropped off the car. My friend dropped me off at home slightly ahead of schedule. I was congratulating myself on my organisation. I felt chirpy. Everything changed when I tried to unlock the door … I could not get into the house because the keys were in the car, back at the garage. I did not have a cell phone and I could not get into the house, so I could not call my friend back.

Heart thumping, I tried to think of a solution. The only option I could see was to ask the gardener to cycle to the garage, to pick up the keys.

I had urged the gardener to return as fast as he could. However, some time passed before he returned. May arrived. We milled about the garden. There was nothing to sit on.

"Humpf!" said May. "This is a fine kettle of fish! Not only can we not have tea, but we cannot even sit down!"

May and I avoided each other for quite a while after that.

May isn't the only person in the family that I cannot get things right with. One of my step-sisters is a stickler for punctuality, and every time I have a date with her, something holds me up. One time a Siamese cat stowed away in the car and I became late by having to return it.

Another time a freak wind blew the tin of cream scones I was taking to our meeting, straight off the bonnet where I had placed it while unlocking the car door. The tin landed upside down causing a chaos of cream and jam, which took some time to remedy.

The last time I had an arrangement with her, she was supposed to follow me to our destination. I set off when I saw her car coming, but lost her after a while.

Later, I discovered that she had a different car, and I had not connected with her at all.

Then there is the case of my mother-in-law, who thinks I am strange and do it on purpose.

Each time I tried to help her something bad happened to me. I got parking tickets on four separate occasions, trying to get her close to places she needed to be. Things fell on me. I was seriously inconvenienced when I was already stressed for time.

Trying to help my mother-in-law prepare for a trip overseas, I had suffered a succession of incidents – two parking tickets, and an unprovoked attack by her suitcase wheels, which I was trying to repair.

A few days before my mother-in-law's return, I went to arrange for the lady who cleaned for her to meet me at her flat, so we could give it a good clean and have things fresh for her return. I had taken down some curtains to wash at home, and needed help rehanging them.

Would you believe it? The lady's dog run out and bit me. Luckily, I was wearing thick denims and it did not break the skin, but it caused a nasty bruise, and was extremely painful. I was assured that the dog had had its rabies shots, at least.

When things go wrong, I go through stages. The first couple of things I shrug off, the next couple annoy me, then I feel sorry for myself (Why me? What did I do to deserve this?). Finally, I get to a stage where the situation begins to seem ridiculous, and I have a laughing fit.

Ted does not understand how I can laugh when things go wrong. When I started to laugh after the dog bit me, he looked nervous and asked me if I wanted some brandy.

In the event, the cleaning lady did not turn up on the appointed day and I had to hang the curtains, clean the flat and plant the colourful flowers I had purchased for the window box on my own, when I was already tired and short of time.

May's Favourite Story

Personally, I did not think what happened was that funny, but every time we discussed the things which happened to me, May brought it up and had another good laugh.

I suffer from sinus, especially during the cold dry part of the year.

One morning, I woke up with a sinus headache. I have found that sometimes placing something warm on my forehead eases the headache. It was cold and I was rather disinclined to get out of bed and prepare a hot water bottle. My eye fell on the mug of hot cocoa, kindly left on my bed side table by my early rising husband.

I felt the mug – too hot to put straight onto my skin. The sheet was not thick enough – I thought in Mama Bear's voice. The duvet was too thick – I thought in papa bear's voice. Ahhh! My t-shirt was just right.

I folded the front of the t-shirt over my head and rested the mug on my forehead. I was enjoying the sensation, when something changed. The heat had changed position. I could not tell right away what was wrong, but something was not right.

I struggled to get the t-shirt off my head with one hand. I did not want to put the mug down until I could see. When I finally emerged, it was to discover that I was holding only the handle of the mug in my fist.

The mug had broken off and fallen into my lap, depositing a large brown mess.

I think this incident was much funnier.

It was Friday lunchtime, and it had been one of those weeks - and one of those days. It was winter. I was stressed and cold. There is something which has the ability to soothe all those ills – COCOA – chocolate and milk – warm and calming. I felt better just thinking about it.

An indication of my brain's level of battering was what happened next. I filled the kettle, placed it carefully in the fridge, and shut the door. Something was not right – I could see a vague reflexion of my puzzled face in the fridge door, as I tried to work it out. Ha! One does not put kettles in the fridge if one wishes them to heat up. One has to plug them into the power supply.

I opened the fridge, removed the kettle and plugged it into its socket. The next step was to spoon cocoa powder into the mug. (This was the instant version – I could not wait for the method which calls for boiling everything up in a saucepan.) Next, I grabbed the kettle and poured water into the mug.

Now what? I tried to stir the powder into the water, and it just was not dissolving. I peered into the cup, trying to work out what was going on. Unfortunately, I got too close to the cup and breathed in dry cocoa powder, which hit the back of my nose, and before I could lift my head, I sneezed directly into the mug.

Cocoa mixture shot out of the cup and splattered into my face.

I went into the bathroom to wash my face. As I bent over the basin, I caught sight of my face in the mirror. It was amazing! The cocoa had distributed itself so evenly that it was just like a face pack. My whole face was chocolate brown, except for the whites of my eyes, and my teeth as I smiled at myself.

By this time, I had been able to work out what the problem had been – I had not let the water boil.

My parents' domestic worker had been ironing in the scullery, and she had witnessed the whole fiasco. African people are extremely polite, and never laugh when someone has an accident or looks silly. However, everyone can be pushed beyond their ability to endure. Poor Spiwe tried her best, but the rest of the afternoon was punctuated by snorts, as she made super human attempts not to laugh, and then exploded when the pressure grew too great.

What Made Louis Laugh

My dad, Louis, did not often laugh out loud. That is not to say that he did not have a sense of humor. He just seldom displayed hilarity. I only ever saw him beside himself with laughter four times.

The first time was when I was about three. I had been on a visit to the UK with my mother, and my father, with half a mind as he shaved in the bathroom, was leading me through a litany of what all the relatives had said.

"What did Granddad say?" "What did Uncle Ron say?" etc

When he got to, "What did Grandma say?" There was no hesitation at all – I really knew the answer to that one. My stepgrandmother had a white Maltese poodle, called Candy, which she treated like a child. A packet of cotton wool was kept on the mantelpiece for the sole use of Candy. I had watched fascinated as Grandma, each time the dog was returned from a walk, took a wad of cotton wool, wiped Candy's bottom and threw the soiled lint into the fire. Grandma always said the same thing to me – and nothing else - that I could recall.

With the exact Yorkshire intonation as Grandma, I said, "Dun't tuch Can-dey!"

Seeing my father laugh until he bent double and then topple into the bath was most gratifying – if somewhat puzzling. After all, I was only telling him the truth.

The next two times were when my younger son was about three.

My mother-in-law baked every week, and put marmalade into things like ginger bread and fruit slices. In order to have a good supply of marmalade, she used to make large quantities of it. The batch in question had been cooked a bit too hot or long, and the peel slithers were hard.

Andy was sitting at the dining room table eating a piece of toast with his Nanna's marmalade spread on it. Seeing him looking glum and pensive, Grandpa asked what was wrong.

Andy answered, "Eating this marmalade is like eating wood sticks," and went back to his task of chewing and thinking.

A few months later, Grandpa was staying with us pending an operation on his varicose veins. Andy listened solemnly while Grandpa made a big production of the procedure. He began by pointing out the offending vessel and tracing its winding path, and informed Andy that it was a worm living in his leg. With many grimaces and extravagant gestures any fisherman would have been proud of, Grandpa described how he was going to the hospital and the doctor was going to give him an injection to put him to sleep. Then he demonstrated how the doctor would make two cuts each end of the unwanted worm and then pull it out (knocking over his tea cup with a particularly violent tugging motion) and sew up the holes.

Andy was obviously not impressed. "Why do not you just take worming tablets?"

The fourth time occurred after I was showing two of my students how to stain slides for the microscope with iodine. Somehow, the iodine bottle slipped out of my hand. It landed upright on the table, but a splodge of iodine shot out of the open end and landed squarely and neatly on my nose. No iodine was spilt anywhere else.

I was playing Kanga in a play of *Winnie the Pooh* at the time – luckily, having a brown mark on my nose would not really matter because I had a shiny black nose painted on for the play.

I rushed to the bathroom to try and remove the stain, which covered my whole nose. I paused only to explain to Louis what had happened, as I passed by his door.

It took me an hour to remove the stain. I tried many different things including, soap and water, face cream and a hard surface cleaner. I eventually succeeded in removing the stain, but I also took off some of the skin.

The bathroom backed onto Louis's lounge/dining room, where he was having lunch. The whole time I was trying to remove the stain I could hear him giving off periodic snorts of laughter.

Somersault, Sneeze and Aggressive Tables

They say children have guardian angels. I feel that I have retained mine. I think she has a wicked sense of humor and is probably unsuited for children – in the same way Shetland ponies are not suitable for children. They look the part, but are so intelligent that they try to scrape riders off with tree branches and such-like things. Not to say that my guardian angel is malevolent in any way – she just enjoys seeing me make a fool of myself.

In the first step class I took at the gym, my legs became tangled up - twice - and I fell off my step onto the carpet in an amalgamate heap. It was in full view of everyone in the class, because I was in the front row. The instructor had a quiet word with me, even before class ended – she suggested I did not try the difficult bits.

Then there was the time I went to draw the curtains in the lounge. Once the curtains were drawn, it was so dark that I could not see where I was going. Somehow, I fell over a coffee table. Once I was launched into the air, I curled myself up for protection. That caused me to do a full somersault, and I landed on my butt, facing in the opposite direction.

Having ascertained that I was completely unharmed, I tried groaning and complaining to attract attention to my (for my age - actually for any age) marvellous feat. Ted was cross the hall playing a game on the computer. After a while, I gave up and went to tell him what had occurred. He grunted and carried on playing his game. What does a girl have to do to get some recognition around here?

A few days later, I was working on the computer, but some mosquitoes had taken up residence under the desk, and were biting my ankles. In annoyance, I drew up my legs and sat cross legged on the chair, so I could keep an eye out for, and swat, any insects intent on drawing my blood.

A sudden, almighty sneeze overtook me. (I am a talented sneezer and my sneezes have been compared to an atomic explosion.) That one was one of my better ones. It lifted me off the chair, and flung me about a meter and a half, into the fireplace.

Ted happened to be going past. "What are you doing?" he said a tad grumpily. (Until recently, Ted had no humor about the things which happened to me.)

"I am sending e-mails," I replied, unfolding myself and returning to the computer.

Quite recently, I was subject to an incident where I was slightly injured. (The only time I have ever broken anything except for my nose, which happened in my childhood, when I fell flat on my face, when the branch I was swinging on came off in my hands.) A small bone was broken between the wrist and little finger of my right hand, and I my arm was in a plaster cast for three weeks. (An incredible inconvenience, which interfered with marking of books, and made me feel as if I had done a day's work, by just getting washed and dressed in the morning.)

I had the privilege of working with a wonderful lady, who is a genius and does amazing things for the theater. We were in the furniture store room of the theater, which had a steep, wooden staircase with no rail, up to a mezzanine arrangement.

We spotted a table in the mezzanine, suitable for dressing the set we were working on. With some difficulty, we extracted it from the bottom of a pile, and decided the best way to get it down was to tip it over, and slide it down the steps.

Having manoeuvred it into place, I was in front and Dorothy was behind. She asked me if I was ready and I said I was, but once she let go, the table proved to be too heavy for me to control, and it began to push me down the stairs.

I started to hurry in front of its relentless pursuit, but it was catching up with me. About a meter and a half from the bottom, I jumped off the stairs. Unfortunately, I could not get my balance and ended up flying through the door, parallel to the floor, nearly a meter up.

The director, in the adjacent rehearsal room, said it was very dramatic. The sound of the table rumbling down the wooded steps sounded just like a drum roll. Then, I flew out of the door, like Superwoman, with my arms stretched out in front, landed flat out, and bounced. I think it was the bounce that caused the injury. My right arm hit the floor and did a reverse windmill move, and my hand chopped the concrete behind me.

People seemed to find this incident excessively amusing. One of my friends, took it upon herself to phone me from Australia – to ask if she had read my message correctly. When I verified the story, she spent the whole twenty minute phone call laughing – no conversation at all!

Thankfully, the guardian angel has been more inventive and less slapstick since then and I have only had a few sudden falls on wet slippery concrete. Judging by the number of times it happens, it's something she simple cannot resist.

The theater put a handrail on the furniture storeroom stairs. They do not want a repeat performance of my grand entrance.

One day, I was giving the cat a saucer of food, when I stepped on the paper the dishes were on. The paper slid, I fell onto the dishes, sending water into the air, showering us both. My head butted into the door, which caught the cat and catapulted him into the passage, slamming shut behind him.

After I cleaned up, I had to feed Taco in the passage, as he refused to renter the kitchen. He was not taking any chances on a repeat performance either. I tried explaining what had happened, but it seems that people are not the only ones to think I make things up.

The Right Price

Something I really appreciate are the little miracles my guardian angel organises from time to time. They cheer me up and make me feel special.

Sometimes they are just for me, but sometimes they enable something I am trying to do for someone else.

The incident I remember best involved my friend's grandparents. My friend, as is the case for many Zimbabweans, was living and working overseas for economic reasons. I had been busy and had not visited her grandparents for some months. When I did go, I was shocked by what I found.

Neither of them had been eating, and they were in quite a state. I decided that they needed one of those powder drinks which build one up during and after serious illnesses. They agreed that that would be a good thing for them, and decided that they would like strawberry flavour.

I only had a certain amount of money, and set out on a hunt. Altogether, I must have gone to six different places, some chemists, some supermarkets. Nearly all of them were out of my price range, and the one place which had a price I could afford did not have strawberry flavour.

I had almost given up, and was going through ways to find a few extra dollars.

My godson was staying with us for a week, and I needed to get some cereal for him before I headed for home. With that end in mind, I made for the nearest supermarket, which was not one I usually frequented.

As I entered the supermarket, I espied a huge block of the food supplement product I had been trying to match my money to. There were rows and rows of it, in all the flavours it came in. Every tin had a neatly printed price on it – too high.

I picked up a tin of strawberry flavour. At first glance, it was no different from its neighbours. There were no dents, no dust, faded label or anything to indicate it was not exactly the same as all the other tins. However, when I turned it around, it had a fresh handwritten price – my price! My heart skipped – that was strange. I checked through the other tins – the one I had in my hand was the only one with a handwritten price that I could find.

Still not believing what had happened, and expecting the till operator to say there was some mistake and charge the higher price, I took the cereal and tin to the check out.

The operator did not react in any way and tapped in the price.

I wondered back to my car, with a beatific smile on my face. Wow! The world was a beautiful place. Is not it amazing how a little miracle can brighten one's life?

"Thank you!"

Things Dropping on My Head

I do not have a large head in relation to the rest of my body, or to most people's bodies, for that matter.

I am not fond of hats. My hair tends to be unruly at the best of times and, if I wear a hat it is just an excuse for my pesky hair to shape itself in a way which makes me look silly when I take the hat off. I have a thin strand of hair almost in the middle of my head which stands straight up in the air, if it is going to rain that day. It is 100% accurate, and I have overheard students discussing the chances of rain, and concluding that they will go and see what my hair is doing. My hair has even been known to rise up en masse, if someone really annoys me and I am trying not to say anything.

Anyway, I digress. What I meant to explain was that wearing a hat would probably help solve the problem I tend to have with birds. I get very nervous when I see birds flying above me, or coming close to me, and have a tendency to be tense, until they have passed on their way out of my air space.

Do not get me wrong, I admire birds and enjoy watching them. All our cats are informed at an early age that birds are not on the menu. They still catch the odd dove and sometimes, even something more exotic but, generally, they humor us in our unreasonable attitude to birds. On occasions, I have rescued birds (sometimes from the very mouths of cats) and even raised nestlings which have fallen from their nests.

Birds, however, do not respect me. Well, perhaps they do, but their ways are not my ways. How do you know what goes through a bird's mind? Whatever, birds are uncannily accurate at dropping bombs, which hit squarely on the top of my head.

Once, I was walking in a quiet back street in Athens. There were apartment buildings on each side of the road. Nobody else was on the street. The sound of traffic was a soft whisper in the distance. Ted's and my footsteps echoed loudly in the silence.

Suddenly, out of the blue, (literally – there was a beautiful strip of Mediterranean blue sky showing between the profiles of the buildings) PLOP! – a large glutinous mass splotched onto my head. It could have been mistaken for the contents of a hen's egg if it was not for the colour and odour.

I never even saw the marksbird responsible.

A few days later, I was admiring a small wee, brown bird in a small tree outside Gatwick airport, in London. It seemed very tame coming right close to me.

"Chirp!" it said as it flew away, leaving a large dropping splattered right across my blouse.

Birds are not the only problem associated with the unusual drawing power of my head. Luckily, it seems to be a particularly hard head.

My head has been hit by a large variety of miscellaneous objects. A cupboard door came off in my hands and fell on it. Once a cat fell out of the top half of a built-in cupboard and landed on it with all claws out. That resulted in an interesting colour job, consisting of spots of red mercurochrome dotted all over my scalp.

One night, drawing the curtains in the lounge started an avalanche of brass candle sticks and other brass artefacts, tumbling off the pelmet. I swear every single one hit me before falling to the floor. There was a slight pause before the last one fell – just to add to the dramatic effect. I had enough bumps, in such an array of sizes, shapes and location, to confuse a phrenologist.

I come up under things, walk or run into walls and doors. Avocado pears fall out of trees – though they seem to have a penchant for the bridge of my nose.

In Germany, on holiday, I was taken on a nature walk in some woods, by my friend. She lead me to a lovely, lofty spreading tree and pointing up, said, "This is a Mirabella - wild plum."

I looked up admiringly, and a plum fell out of the tree straight onto my upturned forehead.

There are so many things I must do, I move from class to class at a pace which is often commented on. Extremely busy, preoccupied and in fast walk mode, I was suddenly and unceremoniously cracked on the head by a large, mean, clay birdfeeder, hanging from the branch of a tree. My knees buckled and I went round in a few circles, like a cartoon character.

The resulting bump took six weeks to subside completely.

My Personal Vacuum

I do not have particularly powerful puff. In fact, when blowing up balloons, it is often a competition as to whether, I am blowing up the balloon or the balloon is blowing up me. When it comes to taking in breath through the mouth, however, I seem to have unusual power. A vacuum seems to be created into which any small object not fastened down is drawn.

The first time I noticed the problem was as a child. When using a peashooter, I had to turn my head way to the side, when taking in air to blow, or the ammunition went straight down my throat. Once, when trying to modify a squib, I swallowed all the gun powder, or whatever you call that grey powder found in fireworks.

As I got older, the objects became bigger and more dangerous to my well being. One Christmas, I took in a deep breath to speak, and swallowed the end of a streamer. This naturally resulted in choking, and my mouth turning an alarming colour due to the dye from the paper. A quick decision had to be made, as to whether, after breaking off the streamer, I should complete the swallowing of what was down, or trying to haul it out. I swallowed it, in the interests of the public good.

My good friend, Liz, and I had a regular date early on a Saturday morning to go jogging. Each week, we took a different route and explored a new area. One Saturday, we were running on a sand road near a poultry farm. It was very pleasant with Msasa trees, birds singing, and the sandy soil was easy on our calves. There was a problem, though. Poultry farms and flies are synonymous.

Naturally, when jogging, one starts to take in more air through the mouth. It was almost inevitable. I took in a deep breath, and a fly went straight down. It was horrible. In the words of a French friend, "It was or-ib-la. You cannot imaginate ow or-ib-la it wos!"

When the second fly went down, I felt really sick, and started to cough. Liz, was not sympathetic. She laughed until she was practically rolling on the ground. Uncharacteristically, I did not have humor about this particular situation. I was beginning to wonder just how good a friend Liz was, between bouts of coughing.

When I got home, I swallowed neat, as an antiseptic, a large slug of the brandy I used to make hot toddies, when Ted or I had flu. As we were due to attend our sons' sports day at school, it was not an ideal solution, so I followed the brandy with a glop of toothpaste. The toothpaste did disguise the aroma of the alcohol somewhat, but not my slightly erratic behaviour.

I had been suffering from a persistent cough which refused to go away. It was accompanied by a runny nose, which required frequent blowing.

Liz and I had arranged a camping holiday in South Africa for our combined families. Liz, who knew many lovely places, chose our route. We stopped in some wonderful scenic, rural areas, with suitable walking and jogging trails for the husbands and us.

At one of the first places, Liz and I set off along a trail. I trotted behind Liz coughing and blowing into the large piece of toilet paper I had equipped myself with for the purpose. As we proceeded, the paper became more and more reduced, soggy and crumbly, until it was just a mass about the size of a heaped tablespoon.

Liz has a terrifying (to me) habit of standing on the edge of sheer drops. I become disorientated and not sure which way up I am, if there is a sheer drop in front of me. My theory is that it has something to do with being dyslexic. One of the theories about the short term memory deficit, common to dyslexic people, is that part of their memory is occupied by trying to keep their balance. If someone else stands on the edges of drops, I feel panic, and imagine them tumbling over the edge.

My brother fell headfirst down a stairwell and was killed in his late thirties, but I was plagued by the dread long before that.

Liz found a drop to stand on the edge of, and I tried not to look at her and ignored her for as long as I was able. When the feelings threatened to overwhelm me, I decided to start walking briskly off down the trail, in the hopes that she would follow me.

It worked. Liz knew exactly what was happening. I kept up the fast pace in case there were any other drops to tempt her.

To my relief, we rounded a bend and saw the camp right below us. All the extra exertion had disturbed my sinuses. I stopped to try and get one last blow out of the lump of tissue. I took a deep breath, and the tissue was not there. A searched of the ground and my clothes, was fruitless . . .

A Hard Decision

It was the Christmas season, and all five of Mary and Mats' sons were coming from overseas. Two of them were married, and my godson had two daughters. There was great excitement. The big problem was that there was not enough space in Mary and Mats' house to sleep everyone, or for the big family reunion Christmas lunch which had been planned.

We have a large house but no relatives, so we offered to open our home both for sleeping accommodation and the lunch. It was a pure delight to have my charming godson and his wife, their two girls and one of the other brothers, stay with us. They are kind, good people in a comfortable, unconscious way which is relaxing and pleasant. All the brothers get on well with each other and treat their parents with consideration.

Our main contribution to the lunch was garlic bread, for which we are famous among our friends, and a non alcoholic fruit punch. Some of the family members did not drink alcohol and the punch was a refreshing drink in the heat for everyone. It had a base of cold green tea, and contained a mixture of pure fruit juices and chopped up fresh fruit. We used only the best ingredients in honour of the occasion, so it was a fairly expensive exercise.

There was a bit of consternation when it was thought that Uncle Al might join us for lunch, and plans to hide the silver were made. As it turned out, he was discouraged to hear that the refreshment offered was a non alcoholic punch, and decided to stay at home in the company of stronger tipple.

A pleasant relaxing time was had by all. A good lunch of cold chicken, mixed cold meats and a large variety of salads, with Christmas cake, ice cream and many other desserts to follow, was consumed. Many loaves of garlic bread were eaten and a goodly quantity of punch was drunk, as well as a small quantity of alcoholic drinks not previously advertised. We danced a bit and sang a bit, and were nice to each other.

On Boxing Day, the immediate family returned for an eat-up-the-leftovers lunch. We had to obtain more ingredients in order to make more garlic bread, as none had survived the previous day. We still had the makings for refreshing the leftover punch, which we had carefully bottled and refrigerated.

Ted was in the scullery, mixing the various components of the punch into the large plastic fish-bowl shaped container we were using for the purpose. He was just putting the finishing touches to the concoction – some sprigs of fresh mint and ice cubes – when a chicken wandered into the room.

"Out! Out!" roared Ted waving his hands about wildly.

Our free range chickens, a motley crew of mixed breeds employed to keep down insects in the garden, were becoming a nuisance. They had taken to entering the house, eating the cats' food, jumping on the work surfaces and leaving unsavoury droppings.

This particular chicken had hysterics when confronted by Ted. It flew into the air and landed in the punch, causing a mini tsunami to splash up the windows and over the work surfaces.

Ted managed to grab the stunned chicken out of the bowl, before it could recover and cause more chaos, and threw it out of the back door.

Then he was faced with a tough decision. What a waste it would be to turf out all those expensive ingredients. Should he still serve the punch and not say anything? There were no obvious avian contributions to the punch. Nobody would know if he did not say anything.

Eventually, sighing in resignation to good sense and ethics, he took the bowl out to the compost heap and emptied it out.

The Detour

One weekend Liz and her family and my family had planned a visit to friends on a farm. However, early on the Saturday morning of the planned outing Liz phoned to say they would not be coming because their car had been stolen during the night. They had all kinds of things to do with police and organising a battery for their other car.

Our family continued with the original plans and had a pleasant day chatting to friends and meeting some new people.

Shortly before we left for home, some neighbours dropped by to borrow a piece of equipment. They were only there for a few minutes. They just happened to mentioned that they had been trying to get through to a family on the phone, to make arrangement about transporting children to school, but could not get hold of them.

It just so happened that I passed the entrance to the farm belonging to the family they were trying to contact, on my way to work. I had noticed the sign because it was eye catching - announcing: "The Bull Pen". The farm was a long narrow strip of land between two parallel roads. A twin of the sign I passed on my way to work was to be found pointing off the wide tar road running parallel to my usual route. I usually avoided the tar road because of the crazy driving indulged in by some of the motorists which used it.

As it would only be a very slight detour from our route home, we offered to deliver a message to "The Bull Pen".

We turned down the dirt road I usually took to work but, though we backed up and travelled the relevant stretch of the road three and four times, we failed to find the sign. Eventually, we decided to cross onto the tar road and see if we could find the other sign.

Sure enough, not far down the tar road we came across the sign. We turned down the road indicated, found the family and delivered the letter.

Soon, we were back on the tar road and heading back to the main road which would take us home. It was an almost dead straight road with wide aprons each side. After we had gone a couple of kilometers, we could see a car parked on the apron ahead.

The thought went through my head that it would be a funny thing if it was Liz's family car, but that would be too farfetched.

As we drew nearer we saw that it was the same make, model and colour as Liz's car. When we were right behind it we realised it was her car!

Ted and the boys piled out to guard the car, while I whizzed off to fetch Liz and her family.

There was nothing missing from the car. The spare wheel and all the tools were still all present. It appeared to have run out of fuel. We towed it home, in jubilation.

What a string of coincidences led to our coming across the car. If the neighbours had come a few minutes later, we would have already left. The name of the farm came up in the few minutes of conversation. I happened to know the sign. We offered to take a message. We could not find the sign (which was back when I went to work on the Monday) so we travelled down the other road.

We had an impromptu party, in celebration.

Rebecca Viljoen

A Real Thai Letter

I have a Thai friend who gets into a lot of trouble. I think she became my friend for the reason that she is prone to strange situations and enjoys funny stories. She was married to an ex English Navy man who also tended to have funny things happen to him.

There are two stories involving Tukita and her husband that I particularly enjoyed.

Once, Tukita and Graham were staying in a caravan. While Tukita was out getting groceries, Graham, in a fit of helpfulness, decided to wash down all the inside surfaces of the caravan. It was really thoughtful of him. Unfortunately, he used the contents of a bucket he thought was soap and water, but turned out to be urine.

My favourite story about Graham took place when he was travelling back on a train, after a picnic with friends. Soon after he sat down he felt something crawling around in his trousers. In order to investigate and get rid of the offending beast or beasts, he entered the WC.

It turned out that the culprits were the proverbial ants, which were in and on his trousers. He decided that the best way to rid himself of the ants was to shake the trousers out of the window. Graham duly removed his trousers and was vigorously shaking them out of the window, when they were suddenly wrenched out of his hands by a train which rushed past in the opposite direction.

When one of Graham's friends finally came looking for him, he opened the door a crack and thrust some money through, with the fiercely whispered directions, "Quick, at the next stop, buy me a pair of trousers size 34! Any colour!"

After I had escorted her back to Thailand after Graham's sudden death from a heart attack, I used to get letters from Tukita in block capitals with no spaces between the letters, no punctuation and incorrectly spelt words . Eg *IAMWALKININARESTARONGTHREEDAISATNIT FROMSEVTOTWEL* (There is a translation at the back of the book if you are a non Tied speaker.) It was wonderful to hear from my friend, but it could take up to three weeks for me to decipher the missives, and even then there would be bits I never worked out. Louis said they were real Thai letters – all the letters were tied together.

I have another special friend, who has as many stories to tell as I do. We can tell each other stories for days and laugh until the tops of our heads hurt.

Tom once saw what must have been two of the last men in London to wear the office uniform of jacket, striped trousers and a bowler hat, and carry *The Times* and an umbrella. They were in the underground having an altercation. Each refused to let the other board the train first. They tried storming through the door side by side without success. Eventually, the train pulled out leaving them both standing on the platform, whereupon they turned on each other, angrily beating each other over the head with their umbrellas.

It came about that, Tom went to visit Tukita, in Thailand. As would be expected, when two such incident prone people got together, things took an unexpected turn. Tom wrote me a letter from them both.

I enjoyed the letter so much, I went to read it to May.

... We were staying on a small farm Tukita has in the country, about 50km from the nearest town, which she runs with her son. Last Tuesday Dang took the car into town to fetch some supplies and did not return.

After three days, we caught a bus into town to see what had happened to him.

We found Dang staying at his friend's house. Dang's friend's father is a doctor and the family lives in a huge modern, double-storey house - but the servants haven't been paid for six months.

The good doctor has a luscious young wife whom he suspects of having an affair, so when Dang went to visit, the father appropriated the car in order to follow the young wife, so that is why Dang did not return.

We are now also staying in the doctor's house, and have been for the last three days. We did not bring any clothes or anything with us to town, but we are managing by borrowing things from the household, and have made a few purchases.

We decided to do some sightseeing while we are here. At first, we planned to go out in the car, but we haven't managed to do that yet. Each time we get ready and are just about to take the car, the good doctor shoots past us, jumps into the car and drives off, giving us a cheery wave. Consequently, we have had to take a bus ...

It was at this point that May exclaimed, "This isn't <u>real</u>, is it?!"

Earrings

It is amazing how a pair of earrings can change the way you appear. My friend, Frances, has hundreds of them. She has them hung on a peg board in little plastic bags.

I have a large number of single earrings with no partners, because I frequently lose one – usually, one of my favourites.

It hardly needs to be mentioned that, I have often inadvertently put on odd earrings – I tell people that it is fashionable - the odd shoes are more difficult to explain.

Earrings are almost as troublesome as I eye glasses in my world. Even preparing the holes to hang them in was an ordeal for me.

I decided to have my ears pierced while visiting Tukita, in Thailand. She took me to a large department store in Bangkok. I was sat on a high stool behind a circular counter. After choosing a pair of silver earrings in a shell pattern, I closed my eyes and waited for the piercing gun.

When some time had passed and nothing had happened, I cautiously opened one eye, to see what was causing the delay. All the conversation was in Thai, so I was not able to follow it. One of the ladies was sharpening the posts on the earrings to a fine point. Another lady approached me, swabbed my earlobes with mentholated spirit, and applied a tea towel holding ice cubes.

When they judged my earlobes to be sufficiently unfeeling, the first earring had its sharpened post thrust through my earlobe. It was not painful, and the ladies put a mirror in front of me, so I could admire their handiwork. This was a mistake. Though, in their defence, the ladies were unaware of a strange reaction I often get when faced with needles and blood. I looked at the thin trickle of blood which ran down and under the earlobe.

There was a blank period and I came too to find myself being supported on the stool by the sales assistants. A large crowd had gathered right around the counter, all talking at the same time. Tukita was running around in circles crying, "A DOCTOR! IS THERE A DOCTOR IN HERE?"

Apparently, I had ground my teeth, gone stiff and appeared to have had a type of fit. Then my eyes had rolled back, and I slumped into a faint.

Everyone was relieved to have me come round and be completely normal. The shop ladies were understandably reluctant to do the other ear, but I assured them it would not happen again, as long as they were quick and did not show me any more blood.

We had to go home after that because I had also wet my pants. I did not really care about fainting but I was unhappy that I had wet my pants, and had to walk to the taxi rank with a ring of friends pressed around me to save me embarrassment.

One windy day, I was walking down the garden path past one of those circular clothes lines which spin around in the wind. The clothes line was empty except for a rag. As I passed by, in a fluke of split second timing, the clothes line span round and the rag caught in my earring and whipped it out. No damaged was caused to my person, and I found the earring, but the butterfly was lost.

The other day, I was in a hurry and put on earrings with butterflies, without looking. When I got to the bathroom to check my appearance, I was not wearing earrings.

Going back to the bedroom, I found both earrings lying on the floor with their butterflies neatly in place. Somehow, in my hurry I had missed the holes in both my ears completely.

Our domestic worker handed me a butterfly fastening that I had lost in the bathroom, when pulling a tracksuit top over my head. The clothing had caught one earring and sent it flying. I soon located the earring but of the butterfly there was no sign. Naturally, I shook out my clothes in case it had lodged there – to no avail.

Mrs K did not find the butterfly in the bathroom. She found it in the spare bedroom – nowhere near the bathroom. How did it get there? Maybe it ricocheted off walls like a miniature golf shot. One can speculate but we will never know for sure.

Tenfold

My boss often used to send me to the bank to get $1 000 in $100 bills. For this exercise, I always took the same sized brown envelope with me.

One day, I trotted into the bank, and into the Priority banking hall, with my usual sized envelope, having warned the bank of my coming. The money was waiting. However, when I came to put the notes into it – they just would not fit. I pushed and folded but they just would not go in. I wondered if the problem was due to the fact that the notes were a new issue. The new denomination was $500, instead of $100. It did not make logical sense because there should be fewer notes.

Eventually, the teller gave me a larger envelope and I went on my way back to the office.

When we came to count the money for distribution, we discovered why I could not fit the notes into the usual envelope – the teller had given me $ 10 000!

May refused to believe this story. "You lie!" she said.

I had to get Ted to verify that he had taken me to the bank on our way home, in order to return $9 000.

The next time I collected money from the bank, they gave me $100 too much.

When I collected the wages a few days later, there was $20 extra. The bank was not interested in us returning $20 and told us to keep it (a crazy inflation was just starting). We bought some snacks and drinks for the office staff.

Rebecca Viljoen

A Medley of Happenings

Reaching for a book I dislodged some magazines, which knocked over a bottle of hand cream, which knocked over a bottle of water, which knocked the fan remote onto the bedside mat. The bedside mat was soft and fluffy, and there were five buttons on the remote, but the fan switched on.

I was talking to a customer who had come to pay a bill. The customer told me how his plaster ceiling had fallen down in the lounge the previous day. I asked if it had become wet in the recent rain storms. He replied that it had not. He thought that it had just got too heavy for the nails holding it up, and had just fallen down.

When the customer had left, I phoned one of my creditors to tell them I had money to pay them.

The lady said that I would never guess what had happened to her the previous day. The plaster ceiling had fallen down in her lounge. I asked if it had got wet; experiencing an eerie feeling of déjà vu, as I took part in the second of two almost identical conversations within half an hour.

"No," she said. "I think they did not put in the right nails and the ceiling just got too heavy for them to hold."

Two plaster ceilings fall down in lounges on opposite sides of the city on the same day, and I speak to both people concerned within half an hour – what are the odds on that?

I was so furious with a politician that I had called down a lightning strike on him.

Next day, to my shock, I read that his house had been struck. I have been very careful about calling down retribution on people since then. I still believed that the politician should be struck by lightning but I do not want to be responsible.

It reminded me of what happened to a work mate. His boss drove him to distraction, and he took to making the toast: "Here's to … … …..'s accident!" every time he had a drink.

One Monday morning, we arrived to find Kenneth looking like a rabbit caught in headlights.

He had been on radio duty over the weekend, and had been on the radio to the boss he had been wishing accidents on for many months, when there was a loud bang and crash, followed by silence.

The boss had been parked on an embankment. A truck had come round the corner and pushed the car over the edge. The boss survived the accident, and the shaken employee stopped toasting altogether.

My New Profession

In order to advertise the production of *Winnie the Pooh* I was playing a part in, the main characters were prevailed upon, on two successive Saturday mornings, to walk through two of the largest malls in the city, dressed in costume and fully made up.

My costume consisted of a hooped cone-shaped main part which hung from my shoulders until it almost brushed the floor. It incorporated a hood with ears, and included mittens. Poking out from under the cone part, were HUGE, LONG, wired feet. The feet were nearly a meter long and, if I was not very careful, had a tendency to get under themselves and ended up in a curled up tangled mass.

The costume had two great advantages. One was that, by bending and straightening my knees, I could whoosh air up and down my body and cool down. (When it is sweltering hot, actors always seem to be called upon to dress in costumes which make them hot enough to require rehydrating solution, and in winter the costumes are so skimpy that the actors are covered in goose bumps, and prone to catching colds and flu.) The other wonder was a MASSIVE pocket, big enough to actually carry Roo, if the material could have stood up to it.

The makeup required a black nose and whiskers. I asked my son, who lived in the UK, if he would send me some face paint. It was not available in Zimbabwe at that time. Unfortunately, he was not able to get it to me in time, but by begging, borrowing and stealing from people with grease paint, I managed to have a nose and whiskers for each show.

The logistics of getting to the promotion venues was quite taxing. I had to get dressed and be transported squashed into the backseat of the car with my costume (with its stiff concentric rings) completely billowed over me so I could not see anything and was nearly smothered.

Fitness was a must for the performance because Kanga had to hop everywhere. Take into account that I was already into my forties, at this point in time. It was December – hot at that time of the year in Southern Africa. At the malls, I was often left behind by the other actors, either getting my breath back after a hopping session, or straightening my tangled feet. When that happened, I dug deep into my pocket, for flyers to distribute. The pocket was wonderful for storing flyers, treasures given into my safekeeping by Roo and Christopher Robin and anything else which required transporting. I still miss that pocket.

At the first mall, one of my pupils spotted me in my kangaroo suit. Her eyes widened in recognition, a look which soon morphed to one of horror appeared on her face, as she turned and sped off - so much for encouraging attendance at the show.

The second mall was much more fun. There was live music, a Father Christmas giving out sweets and a children's play gym, where a birthday party was in progress. Father Christmas and I did an exchange – he gave me sweets, which I popped into my pocket and I gave him a flyer.

At the birthday party, we were given a large glutinous slice of chocolate birthday cake. The others had a couple of bites and left the rest, it being too problematic to carry around. I wrapped my slice up carefully in paper serviettes and put it in my pocket.

An ex-boss was at the mall. When he recognised me, he laughed himself silly, pointing at me and holding his stomach – very rude. Fortunately, I am immune to being laughed at, in fact, there must be a bit of the stand up comic in my make up, because I get pleasure from cheering people up.

I had a dance with the band and some kids.

Finally, we were free to go. Roo's parents were late in fetching him, and he was tearful. I wiped his face with tissues from the pocket. I gave him a Father Christmas sweet to suck, from the pocket. He was quiet for a while, but when his parents still had not come after twenty minutes, he began to complain, and wailed that he was hungry. I asked him if he would like a slice of chocolate cake. He looked at me blankly. Obviously, he was wondering where the chocolate cake was going to come from. I began to rummage in my pocket.

"You have chocolate cake in there?!" he exclaimed in amazement.

I produced the cake only slightly squashed at the edges but still wrapped up securely, and handed it over. Cake consumption kept Roo thoughtfully busy, until his apologetic parents bustled up at last.

Four months later, my son had come for a visit. Just before we were about to take him to the airport for his return, he handed me a packet of face paints. I thanked him, as was appropriate, but it did go through my head that I did not really have a use for them anymore.

Feeling sad, not knowing when I would next see my son, we returned home after seeing him off. As I entered the door, the phone was ringing.

"Hello?" said a lady's voice. "Is that Rebecca Viljoen?"

"Yes," I answered cautiously, not recognising the voice and a little wary due to previous experiences with phone calls.

"Ha!" said the voice. "I wish to hire you in your professional capacity."

My mind could not think what that might mean. Oh my hat! Surely not The Profession! It was going to be one of those calls – I was already beginning to feel disorientated.

As it turned out, the lady was the manager of the fun mall. She had seen me interact with the kids during our *Winnie the Pooh* promotion, and was offering me a stint as the Easter Bunny.

I took the job, and had an interesting morning in the mall.

Being paid has made me a professional actor, and eligible to join an actor's union. The main reason I took the job, however, was that it required the use of face paint - I took it as a sign that I had just received a packet.

Nanu Nanu

Due to a number of physical anomalies, I often joke that I do not come from this planet. I am allergic to snow. My hands go as red as a tomato, and I can feel the heat coming off them from as far away as I can get them from my face. Tea, milk, sugar, preservatives and other food additives are perceived by my body to be alien substances requiring its intervention. Strange things happen to me and, occasionally, to those around me.

I am not ill often, touch wood, but when I am, I frequently have symptoms that baffle doctors into actually admitting that they are baffled. It isn't comforting to know that you have an "interesting rash" or that your heart and breathing inter react and, especially, to hear that the doctor has no idea what is wrong with you.

Some years back, I developed some sharp pains in various areas of my body, and was sent to a specialist. The specialist asked me if I had a pain in my butt! I was not sure at first if he was speaking metaphorically or physically. I gave him a hard stare. It just so happened that one of the places I did have bad pain was in the buttocks.

Apparently, that is how you distinguish *spongio anthropy* from other diseases. It's par for the course to get something where the doctor asks if one has a pain in the nether regions, as part of the diagnosis, I suppose.

I also have a simian line (instead of a heart and head line, there is one line which goes straight across the palm). I am dyslexic, dyspraxic, slightly autistic and ADHD and an Aquarian – so the wacky odds are stacked against me.

What really disturbs me is that I have twice been told by complete strangers that they are truly from another planet. The reason they would do such a thing is food for thought. Do they recognise something familiar in me, like that sign I am sure is across my forehead which encourages people who want favours, and beggars, to be sure I am the one to approach?

I think, the first man to tell me he was from another planet, was just trying to throw people. I professed, and was, very interested in the man's planet. I asked its name and about its climate, vegetation, political systems and fauna. Then I asked how he came to be on earth, and what he was doing here. I cannot remember what he said, but we both had an enjoyable time discussing it. He always greeted me with his planet's greeting shake, whenever we met after that.

The second encounter was completely unexpected. We had had a burglary and an insurance assessor come to investigate our claim. I was all set for a fairly boring afternoon, when the man suddenly, without warning, announced that he came from another planet.

I was completely taken back by such a sudden deviation of subject, not to mention content. Falling back on my previous experience, I decided to carry on as if the man had said nothing out of the ordinary. This time, I opened by asking him how he knew, and if there were others on earth.

Apparently, he had been hypnotised and there were others but I cannot recall why. That time I was not so entertained by the conversation - actually quite bothered. Once you can shrug off, but a second encounter is worrying, and the man was obviously completely serious.

I wished now that I had asked him why he had told me.

The Puzzle to the Keys

Anybody who has ever been in charge of a key or bunch of keys has lost them at some stage. I have special places where I keep keys, but sometimes when I am in a hurry I put them in a different place to the one I intended – the wrong drawer for instance. I lost a set of car keys in the house some years ago – I know it was in the house. They resurfaced recently in a cardboard box in the school storeroom, but the car they belonged to has long since been sold.

I have been involved in two incidents where keys have miraculously been found before I knew they were lost.

Once a group of friends and I were staying in the mountains. We decided to try and follow a stream up a mountain to its source. There were no paths, so we were tromping about in some tall weeds with some tenacious and irritating seeds which stuck all over us.

Eventually, after some hours we were hot and sticky and dirty and decided to give up our quest, and return to the chalet.

Suddenly, one of the party held up my set of car keys. By some miracle, he had crossed over the place where they had dropped unnoticed from my pocket, onto one of the few bald spots on the whole mountainside.

It would have an unmitigated disaster if we had lost those keys, and it would have put a serious blight on our holiday. As it was, we felt even more upbeat, and felt smiled upon by a benevolent and caring power who was blessing our holiday.

The second incident was even more bizarre. Once again it was associated with another long looked forward to, desperately needed, break.

A friend had come from Switzerland and she, Frances and I were going shopping to get supplies for our stay on an island in Lake Kariba. I was busy arranging my escape from school for a few days. Frances was busy packing and doing last minute e-mails and tidying. Alex was pottering about doing her things, and it was proving difficult for us to all be in the same place at the same time. However, we eventually made a time and began to assemble at the gate.

Alex, who was sporting an orthopaedic shoe, having kicked her instructor a little too hard during a karate training session and breaking some toes, was ensconced in the back seat of Frances's car, which Frances had parked in front of the gate, ready to drive out.

As I hurried up, Frances was just about to open the gate. What happened next was completely amazing to Alex, sitting in the car. She was not able to hear any of the words spoken over the sound of the car engine. What she observed was a strange mime.

Suddenly, Frances stopped opening the gate and made some angry gestures. She felt her butt and made some more angry gestures. She then beckoned to me, stuck out her nether regions in my direction and imperiously pointed to them. I cautiously approached said region with my nose foremost. After drawing well within Frances's personal space I stepped back and nodded my head. Alex gazed on mystified, unable to think of any reason why we would be behaving in such an incomprehensible and unexpected manner.

What was actually taking place was something along these lines.

Frances: (Gesticulating angrily) My butt is wet! I am sure it is a cat again. I bet a cat has weed on my car seat! Again! (Sticking out butt) Smell my butt!

Rebecca: (Sniffing the offending area gently, stepping back and nodding.) That is definitely cat wee.

After a few more recriminations etc we were all, finally, seated in the car. Frances decided that, as we were running so late and she did not have time to deal with the abused car seat, or her soaked by proximity bottom, she would open and close the gate in order to air things as much as possible.

We turned right and drove about a hundred meters to the T-junction. At the T-junction we turned left. From there we proceeded a block to the next intersection, negotiating a speed hump on the way. We turned right at the intersection and drove about ¼ kilometer to the vegetable and food market where we hoped to make some purchases. Unfortunately, they had closed five minutes before we got there, so we turned into their entrance and reversed out to face back down the road we had just travelled.

We were roaring down the road on our way to a large supermarket, when there was a scraping noise and something flew through the window and landed with a thunk in the back, at Alex's feet.

To our amazement, the object which had flown through the window proved to be the gate keys which Frances must have left on the roof of the car. They had remained on the roof throughout all our manoeuvres and then shot through the window, instead of flying off into the wild blue yonder.

There was a sequel to the mime. One night on the island we were preparing for bed. Alex had already got into bed and had tucked the mosquito net around her. Suddenly, she started doing strange contortions and muttering and, finally, rocketed out from under her mosquito net. I had been watching her and wondering what unwanted creature had joined her in bed.

"Stinky stink bug!" she complained. "It is somewhere in my hair! Smell my hair!" she demanded, sticking her head in my face.

I have close friends I love them dearly and I would do anything for them, as I am sure they would for me. It's not just anyone you can ask to smell unpleasant things on your butt or your hair. However, it certainly is the other side of friendship.

A Relaxing Bath

I decided to have a relaxing bath after a stressful week. I ran a deep hottish bath. To assist me to achieve the desired level of calm, I took an interesting book and a small glass of red wine into the bathroom with me. It was not dark enough for candles.

Settling myself comfortably into the bath, I leant back sighing with contentment, the book in one hand and the glass of wine in the other. After taking a sip of wine, I stretched out my arm to place the glass on the side of the bath. I had reached an exciting part in the story, and my nose remained glued firmly in the book, so I was not looking what I was doing and managed to drop the glass over the edge of the bath.

The glass fell about 40cm onto the carpet tiles and came to rest on its side. Its mouth was facing away from the bath. Most of the wine spread in a puddle around the glass. I stomped out of the bath and mopped up as much of the wine as I could, drank the dregs from the unbroken glass, and spread the damp floor cloth over the stain, so it could draw up the wine. I returned to the bath water and my book.

That is when I saw it. My eyes slowly travelled from about a meter and a half up the wall – continuing upward another meter, nearly to the ceiling. I lay gazing for some minutes in disbelief. There was red wine running down the walls from splashes on three walls!

My initial wonder was where the force came from to send the wine two and a half meters into the air – but there was a farther mystery.

There were no wine splashes on anything below where the splashes started on the wall. There were wickerwork shelves about a meter high holding towels, on the wall across from the bath. On the wall behind me was a stool bearing the clean clothes I intended to wear after I had had my bath. Behind the bath was a tiled area bearing toiletries and a large plant. None of these bore any visible wine splatter.

I called for my husband to come quickly because something terrible had happened. When he came, he looked at the wine splattered walls and, without comment, began to clean up the mess.

When I pressed him for a comment, he said, "I thought something had happened to the plumbing."

"But…" I said, waving my arm to indicate the affected walls. "How…?"

"You failed to take into account that it happened to you," was all he would say.

I asked a maths teacher to try and explain what happened. His conclusion – I give out a force field!

The Case against Rattler

Rattler was the name I gave my bike when I was a teenager. I desperately wanted a horse, but there was no sign that a horse was ever going to be mine. I had wanted a piano when I was younger, but I had never got one of those either. My mother liked to use my desires as bargaining points to get what she wanted. I expect nothing came up big enough to warrant a piano or a pony.

One Christmas I had almost persuaded my mother into getting me a donkey, but while we were engaged in negotiations with the man who owned the donkeys, a dog had suddenly raced up and bitten into my mother's calf. A man with a muzzle in hot pursuit of the dog, grabbed it, made it let go and muzzled it, before it could do more damage. He was most apologetic and explained that he had just taken the dog's muzzle off so it could eat its dinner.

My mother had to drive to the hospital for a tetanus shot and a few stitches. I dare not mention donkeys after that.

Rattler looked nothing like a horse; for a start, he was green. He rattled right from the start, even thought he was bought brand new from the Greek man at the corner store, Mr Buzzoni.

I decided to pretend he was a horse. I do not know quite what the bike objected to; the name or being transformed into a horse, but it took to throwing me over its handlebars and doing other bizarre things to me. The timing was too perfect to be coincidence. My Geography teacher said I should have a merit badge for my bicycle riding. I do not think any of the incidences he witnessed had anything to do with me. That bike was inhabited by something.

Once when I was late for school, I nearly killed the Geography teacher when I came whizzing around a corner and the bike went right for him. I only just managed to steer clear of him at the last moment. The bike did not slow down at all but sped me towards school and turned right into the gate, hitting the same stone it hit nearly every morning with its outside pedal. If it hit the stone with the inside pedal doing that right turn, I would agree that it could be my fault cutting the corner too sharply. However, it was on the other side and surprised me every time. The pedal became bent right up after a while, and uncomfortable to operate.

On another occasion, I was cycling past the Geography teacher with a goose in a cardboard box on the carrier. Just as I drew level with the man, the goose somehow got its head and neck out of the box, and proceeded to peck viciously at the part of my anatomy most easily in its reach – my butt. Embarrassed, I tried to pretend that nothing untoward was happening, and continued cycling until I was out of sight of his amazed gaze.

The Geography teacher was the owner of a Honda 50cc motor cycle. Rattler had no gears and was quite hard work to pedal up hills. A friend loaned me their three speed bike one day, and I flew up a hill. It just so happened that the Geography teacher was traversing the same hill on his Honda 50cc. I do not know which one of us was more taken back when I overtook him, and left him standing.

One day, I was riding Rattler down a hill on that same road. I noticed that the front mudguard was sticking out to one side. I put my foot out to straighten it. Before I could do anything, my foot was grabbed by the spokes of the front wheel. My leg was yanked forward by the momentum and I flew over the handlebars. My foot came to rest on the ground and the back of the bike somersaulted over itself and landed resting on its seat and handlebars. Miraculously, I was entirely uninjured. The same cannot be said for Rattler. He had seven broken spokes and the front rim was so bent that I had to walk him home holding the front wheel off the ground

There was a dip in our drive made as it left the tarred road. A few weeks after he recovered from the accident to his front wheel, I made a quick trip to the nearby shops on Rattler. In front of the shops was an open parking area. There was a single 50mm diameter pole, marking the beginning of the cycle track. On the way home, I waved to my friend's brother and Rattler mortified me by running straight into the only obstacle in the whole space.

I could not wait to get my blushing face off the street. As we swooped off the road into the dip in our drive, Rattler picked up a thick piece of wire, which I swear had not been there 15 minutes before. The wire jammed his front wheel to a halt, and I was catapulted over the handlebars.

Once again I was unhurt, but Rattler did not give up. He ran me up wire netting, and threw me into ditches. He deliberately slowed down when I put my feet on his handlebars, so we nearly toppled over into the mouth of a dog which kept running out of its yard on my route to and from school, to chase me.

While on a holiday in Germany, I rode many different bikes recklessly up and down mountains without mishap. The only incidents in a whole month were when I nearly ran over a suicidal cat, which gazed at me mesmerized as I waved my arms shouting, *"Achtung! Achtung!"*; and having the bottom of one leg of my stretch pants ripped off by a jutting stick, on an opportunist tree stump.

I rest my case.

Rebecca Viljoen

Car Trouble

The clutch on the car was slipping. Eventually, Ted decided that we needed a new clutch cable. I was eight months pregnant at the time. I was instructed to go into town and purchase a new one. Ted gave me the names and addresses of two parts shops to try.

I jerked and screeched my way into town, dreading each time I had to stop at a light and start off again. The first shop I tried to find was on a one way street. I had to traverse the whole town to get onto it. After doing two whole circuits of the town, and not finding the shop, I decided to give up and try and find the other shop.

I had no trouble locating the building, which had a huge sign. I found a parking and walked to the building. Spotting a large sign proclaiming "SPARES", I approached it, only to discover a smaller sign which informed me "We have moved".

I left the building which had been vacated by the motor people and was awaiting transformation into a mall. Looking about, I saw another parts shop. Unfortunately, they were unable to supply the desired part, but directed me to another shop.

It involved walking about three blocks, but I found the place without too much hassle. Spotting a large sign bearing the words "SPARES" near the back of the shop, I made my way towards it.

When I got closer, there was a small sign saying: "We have moved", followed by directions. It was getting tedious.

I made my way most of the way round two sides of a block and found the new place. To one side was a large sign declaring "SPARES". I walked towards it. As I got closer, there was . . . no, not another sign. There were two people in the line in front of me, wearing overalls. One from each of the companies I had failed to find.

When I finally returned home, clutching the new clutch cable, Ted climbed under the car and discovered that we did not need it! Part of the plate had bent. It was bent back and pop riveted in place and everything was hunky dory.

A few days later, I was sitting on the lawn, when I noticed that the inside tread of two tyres on the car was worn right down. I told Ted, who could not have got far enough down, because he thought I was imagining things.

The next day, I was turning into the car park of the supermarket, when I heard a hissing sound. I had some trouble locating its origin at first. However, as I got out of the car I was just in time to witness the last of the air escaping from one of the suspect tyres. I had a flat.

Luckily, two kind African gentlemen came to my rescue. None of us was very sure what we were doing. By trial and error, we located all the necessary tools and discovered that the spare tyre lived in a bracket at the front with the number plate attached. Once a bolt was unscrewed, the bracket swung to the ground.

With the spare in place and the flat in the bracket, I thanked the kind men and did my shopping.

As I drove into our gate, the car hit a bump. There was a thump and a very alarming metallic sound. I stopped the car and got out. We could not have secured the bracket properly because going over the bump had shaken it loose and it had dropped down and been bent over to one side, where it was obstructing the free movement of one of the wheels. Normally, I would have been aghast at what I had wrought, but my anger turned on Ted, because I had told him of the danger the condition of the tyre represented, and I had to deal with the consequences.

There was nobody around to help me this time and I had to fetch Ted from work. I did the only thing I could think of. I lay on the ground, big tummy and all, and forced the bracket away from the tyre with my feet. Shifting my position for the right leverage, I then jammed the bracket upwards, so it was sort of in the right place, and secured it.

I complained bitterly to Ted, but as was his way, he ignored me. I finished my tirade by pointing dramatically to the other tyre and said, ". . . and that will be the next one!"

That night we had arranged to visit friends. We had a very pleasant evening, and it was past midnight when we left for home.

Halfway back, I heard the now familiar hissing sound. We did not have a spare because the other tyre was too damaged to repair, and we had not had time to purchase a new one. There was nothing to do but park the car, and walk the rest of the way home.

The following day, Ted had obtained two new tyres and prevailed upon a friend to drive us to the car. After the tyres had been changed, Ted drove off with his friend, and left me to return with our car. I put the key in the ignition and turned it and . . . the key broke off in the lock.

I had quite a few frustrating experiences with that car. It often developed sudden mechanical faults.

Once I backed it into the side of the house when trying to manoeuvre between the shed and a tree with a swing. I'm not sure quite how it happened because the shed and the tree were so far from the house that you would not think it possible. All I know is that, suddenly, I was revving and getting nowhere and when I looked back, I was trying to push the house over – there was not even a jolt when the car and the wall connected.

Another time, I complained to Ted, for about two months about the squishy brakes. Then, one day, I went through an intersection because they failed completely. I was not amused and accused Ted of trying to kill me. He said I was being dramatic!

What was dramatic for me was what happened because the battery was flat. For about a month I had to get help off the street and from the cook next door, to push start the car every time I had to go out.

Then came the day when the cook, a stranger and I were pushing the car backwards down the drive, so that we could get a good run up. I had the driver's door open, as I was pushing too, up the slight slope. Glancing back, I realised we were too close to an avocado tree, and if we carried on the door would be bent backwards. I shouted, "Stop! Stop!" but the two men were too busy chatting to hear me. I stopped pushing and tried to pull, but the car and I were no match for the power of the two men, who continued to talk and just put in more effort when they felt resistance. We went past the tree and the door was bent right back against the front wing. There was not much visible damage but the door made terrible grating sounds when opened and closed.

It was like that for a couple of weeks. Then one day, I was in a roaring hurry because I was late for a dentist appointment. I rushed up to the car, pulled open the door, and the whole thing, came off in my hands and dropped to the ground.

On the way back from the dentist, I stopped to pick up some meat from my step brother's butchery. I had to climb out of the passenger door. When asked why I had exited through the passenger door, I explained what had happened. My brother said he happened to have a spare battery, which he sold to me and fitted.

When I told Ted I had bought a new battery, he was cross. He said he could buy batteries cheaper! Besides, he continued, how did I know that the problem was the battery.

The car did not need to be push started the next morning.

Pathologically Unsuited

Toothpaste and citrus fruit have it in for me. They both squirt me in the eye with their juices at every opportunity. The other day, I was sitting next to someone who was dealing with a grapefruit and was squirted in the eye! It is irritating. Glasses are good protection from such actions, but as I only use glasses for reading, I am not usually wearing them when brushing my teeth or eating oranges, or sitting next to people eating citrus, for that matter.

Door handles are almost as bad. Their persistent grabbing seems to be directly proportional to my level of stress. I will be minding my own business walking along the passage or somewhere, when I am rudely jerked to a halt, due to being attached to a door handle by some part of my clothing, and given a painful battering by a swinging door.

Once, Tasha, my friend's Yorkshire terrier and I were walking peacefully and sedately along, when I was ambushed by a door handle. In a fraction of a second peace became pandemonium, as Tasha got tangled in my feet at the same time. Tasha was squeaking and I was squeaking as we madly tried to avoid being in the same space at the same time, while the door swung backwards and forwards knocking both of us off balance at every opportunity.

To make things worse, I got the giggles when I heard May ask Louis, "For goodness sake! What is that girl doing NOW?"

Cord, string or other snaky shaped object are a nuisance but my biggest bug bear is spectacles. They pile up on my head (people ask me if I know I have three pairs on my head. I say I do, but I am usually lying. They shed arms (then they won't sit straight and make everything look squiffy and keep falling off) they hide and generally torment me. I catch my fingers in them when I am gesticulating, so they fly off at inopportune moments, especially when I am teaching. Sometimes I sit on them or tread on them when they drop, so they become mangled and distorted, and do not let me see important things.

I tried hanging them around my neck with cord, but that only made things worse. I caught my fingers in them more often and nearly throttled myself.

I have found my glasses in the washing machine, the freezer and fridge and other unexpected places, that I do not usually think to look in when they are lost. I tried having extra pairs, but visiting friends borrow them and have a tendency to absentmindedly take them home with them.

After going to a meeting one night, I was not able to find my glasses. I phoned my hostess to enquire, but she said that they were nowhere in sight. I had to buy another pair.

A couple of weeks later, the lady phone me up to say she had found my glasses. She was in the dog kennel (I do not know what she was doing in there) and had discovered that her dog (a very supercilious, studious looking canine) had appropriated them in their case, and had been spending his spare time whittling away at the case with his teeth. Probably, he was trying to get at the glasses in order to wear them – I think they would have suited him.

On another occasion, I had been marking and went to open the gate for Ted. By the time I got back inside, my glasses had disappeared. I turned the place upside down to no avail.

It was most inconvenient. I was stage managing a production of *Antegone* and was supposed to give sound cues at the rehearsal that night, but I could not see where we were on the script. Consequently, I had to make mad guesses, based on who was where and what I could glean from the actors who came off stage. Needless to say, it was chaotic.

For the next rehearsal, I borrowed an old pair of Louis's glasses. At least I could follow the script. However, they did not suit me and people made rude comments.

I bought a new pair of glasses.

For the next three weeks friends who visited the house, the staff, their children and my family and I, made daily searches in the garden.

Finally, one of the children found the glasses in a flower bed – with the cord still intact.

Even considering what trouble spectacles are, contact lenses would be even worse. I would end up tiddly-winking them far and wide and probably end up swallowing them or something.

It is a pity I cannot do without glasses because I am pathologically unsuited to them.

How Fashion Is Born

The school office is a hive of activity. My desk sits in the middle of the floor. That particular day it was covered by a tablecloth which matched the curtains. The curtains could be described as sun filter but they have vertical lines of an open weave pattern alternating with the ordinary closed weave texture lines. I am always trying to do at least four things at once and am continually jumping off my seat to do something.

That morning, I was wearing a pair of three quarter jeans with a line of three buttons sewn vertically down the outside of each calf. As usual, I was trying to mark books, find files, do photocopying, explain Maths problems and answer a variety of queries. After a period of marking, I jumped up to do some photocopying and everything was swept off the table, because the table cloth was attached to the buttons on one of my calves. I detached myself and replaced everything on the table.

After a while, I was back at my desk and worked away until the next interruption required me to leave my desk. I rushed off in another direction and once again everything flew off the desk, because the tablecloth was once again attached to me.

When I returned to my desk, I moved my chair to the side of the desk because the tablecloth was shorter on the sides. It was to no avail. The next time I got up I was attached once again. This time I managed to stop moving before everything followed me.

During the morning, I became attached twice more. I started working on another desk, but as I was passing my desk after lunch, the secretary saw the table cloth flow out and attach itself once again.

That was the last straw and I changed the table cloth.

One of the teachers commented that the message was obvious. . . I should have been wearing the tablecloth!

Strings and Things

In order to keep a record of times and what was being taught, teachers who tutored were required to write their hours and comments in the Tutor Record Book, which was located on a corner of my desk. One day, causing great inconvenience, because we were not able to reconcile the hours and payments, the record book disappeared and was never seen again. None of the ensuing enquiries produced any clues as to what had happened or who could have taken it.

In an effort to prevent a repeat of the incident, I attached a long piece of thick string to the book and tied it firmly to a front leg of my desk. The only problem was that every time I approached that corner of the desk, the string became wrapped around my ankles. Nobody else seemed to have the problem but it happened to me on numerous occasions. Sometimes I would be out of the nearby door before I realised I was caught again.

The culmination came one afternoon when I was tutoring a student. I was wearing thick denims. I picked up a worksheet and took three paces to the end of the table where my student was seated. At that point, the unnoticed string tightened and I was felled like a tree - going down so suddenly that I still had the worksheet held in my hands in front of me.

I untied the string from the front leg of the desk and tied it to the back leg. That seems to have solved the problem.

Things like that seem to happen when I am particularly stressed, though having said that, any string-shaped material (or sticks) have an affinity for my ankles and toes at all times. Inanimate objects either attach themselves to me or fly away from me in times of stress.

One day after tidying my desk, I walked away, to find a wire filing basket attached to the right pocket of my cotton jeans.

On examination, it turned out that there was a break in one of the wires of the filing basket, but the gap was very narrow. How the material of the pocket managed to slip through the gap is question enough, but I had been standing, so the level of the pocket was above the desk and the filing basket and the pocket opening was facing backwards. Whichever way I had turned from the desk, the basket would have been presented with the closed side of the pocket. I had not lifted the basket, only rearranged the papers that had been in it.

Stationery as a class seems to be trying to avoid me. I cannot keep a pen, pencil, sharpener, eraser, ruler or whatever for long. Important bits of paper disappear, often forever.

One day, I was driving with one of my mature students – I was going past her home on my way to the theater. Morag was reading an e-mail. When I stopped at a stop street, the e-mail flew out of the open window. We pulled over and searched the area for ten minutes, but failed to find the missing paper. After five minutes, Morag, who had witnessed a number of my incidents, was bent over double with laughter. She thought I was the cause of what happened.

One of my lovely friends, who live out of town, often used to invite me to join her on her errands when she came into town, and to have tea or coffee somewhere. She does not ask me so frequently these days. I cannot help but wonder if it has something to do with the things which took place when I was with her.

On one occasion, we pulled into a supermarket car park and a runaway trolley ran straight for us. We had to leap out of the car smartly and only just managed to catch it before it crashed into the side of the car.

Another day we were being pursued down the road by a large dog intent on biting the tyres and ripping off the wing mirrors. As she did some tricky manoeuvres to avoid damage both to the car and the dog, my friend commented, "These things only happen to me when I am out with you."

Another thing with suspect motives is my electric hair remover. It is an efficient little machine, but it has some quirks. The mechanism consists of a little motor which circulates some springs, which cunningly entrap hairs and yank them out by the roots. Yes, it is quite torturous, but no more than most beauty treatments in my experience.

In the process of removing unwanted hairs from various places on my body, I have found that the machine is ambitious and sometimes, when I am not paying proper attention, leaves its job with small hairs and tries to go for the bigger hair on my head. This always results in it becoming horribly tangled up, and depending on where it has climbed, I sometimes have to ask a third party to help me get it out. More than once, it has had to be cut out and the hairs foaming around its mouth extricated hair by hair.

Its worst foray occurred the day I decided to use it to remove some hairs from the tops of my thighs. I should have known better. It grabbed onto some pubic hairs and before I could stop it, had made itself a cosy nest.

It took a painful twenty minutes to extract it from my pubic hair. There was no way I was going to ask for help extracting it from there.

Changing a Light Bulb

The X Factor can work its way into any activity. The most mundane task can build up into a bizarre experience.

One day I decided to change the light bulb on the security light by the front door. There were three men in the house, but everyone was ignoring it. Maybe they knew what it would entail.

There was a flower tub under the light with large spiky sisal plants all round it. I climbed onto the flower tub and examined the light fitting. One particularly bad tempered sisal plant spitefully jabbed at my ankles. The fitting was a coach lamp which was not well designed – the bulb did not fit through the opening at the bottom and required the unscrewing of four screws to remove the bottom half. I went off to get a screwdriver.

Balancing precariously on the sides of the flower tub, I started on the first screw. The sisal plant continued its vicious attack on my ankles and dribbles of blood ran down both ankles. A screw came loose and dropped out and was swallowed up by the sisal plant.

I wrestled with the next screw, but despite my determination and care, that screw was also gobbled up by the greedy sisal plant. Exasperation rose in me as I started on the third screw, augmented by the hostile sisal plant's constant prodding.

When the third screw fell and was also swallowed up by the plant, followed by the screwdriver, which slipped out of my hand. I was incensed.

I stomped off to the shed and armed myself with a *budza*. Taking great swings, I launched a furious attack on the provoking sisal plant. Suddenly, one of the blows missed and I lost my balance and began to fall forward, the *budza* completing its swing between my legs. The sisal plant held up a hand with pointed nails and I saw spikes looming closer – right in line to pierce my eyes.

With super human effort, I threw my weight backwards. The spiked claws receded from my sight. However, I then I had another problem. I could not get my balance because the *budza* was between my legs. As I staggered down the drive, the *budza* travelled from thigh to ankle and back down again, hitting first one leg, then the other.

I was about ten meters down the drive before I finally managed to stabilise.

My husband, who was working on his bench nearby, looked up and said, "It is enough to make a cat laugh," and went back to what he was doing.

I went back to what I was doing and completed the destruction of the sisal plant. Finally, I managed to retrieve the screw driver. The screws were lost forever. After replacing the light bulb, I had to scratch through the piles of assorted nails and screws which littered the shed floor for replacements.

The next job was to apply arnica to the collection of bruises which decorated the inside of my legs, from thigh to ankle.

How many blonds does it take to change a light bulb? I'm not blond, by the way - pity, I could have used the help.

Gravity

Once I was sitting in an office, on one of those office chairs which can be made higher or lowered by twisting the seat on its spiral. I was tapping away on the computer with great concentration, when the screen disappeared. It just vanished into thin air leaving a dark hole.

I was mystified until I realised that I was lying flat on my back on the carpet and I could not see anything because my head was inside a metal waste paper bin.

The top of the chair had fallen off its spiral. It had all happened so fast that I had no recollection of the time between sitting typing and landing on the floor. It is possibly a result of being *dyspraxic*, where your brain and body are not well connected.

We have all heard of the falling apple which alerted Isaac Newton to the force which pulls things down. Gravity is the force which pulls you towards the centre of the earth. There is also a pull between all solid objects, which is the reason we circle around the sun and neither get sucked into it or sail off into space.

Gravity is an insidious thing. Have you noticed how big the spaces are between light posts and power poles and how small the width of the poles compared to those spaces? You may also have noticed how often motorists wrap themselves around the poles.

One of these days I am going to do a scientific experiment with security bars and prune pips. It seems to me that the number of times pips bounce off bars instead of sailing through the much larger gaps is out of all proportion to what one would expect.

Well, that force appears to have set its sights on me.

The number of times I have suddenly found my feet no longer supporting me is more than I can count. There are two distinct fall patterns. Either I slip suddenly and am on the ground without any awareness of the time between standing and lying, or I swan about very gracefully until the gravity gets me completely off balance and I collapse on the ground in a tangled heap with my limbs wrapped around each other like spaghetti.

Once I was working at a desk which had its left side pressed against the wall and children's desks facing into the front and the right side. I leaned forward tipping my chair, in order to look at a book on the desk of the child in front of me. The chair became a slide and I was tipped under the desk. The chair back followed me under the table, effectively caging me under the desk. To my surprise, the children did not fall off their chairs laughing, but said they were sorry.

Another time students surprised me with their reaction was the time I fell into the sports cupboard. We keep our sports equipment in a cupboard which can be used as a seat. It has large lids which you lift in order to access the equipment. One day a student came to get a tennis ball during a lesson with some senior students.

I was holding up a lid with my left arm while fishing about in the bowels of the cupboard with my right, when my assistant took hold of the lid with the words, "Let me hold that for you."

Unfortunately, the few centimeters my assistant pushed the lid back threw me off balance and I did a slow pirouette and fell backwards into the deep cupboard with my legs hanging over the side.

I sat up to see why there was dead silence. All I could see was a sea of faces with big round eyes. This just increased my giggles to the point where I was unable to get out of the cupboard.

All I can say is that the students I teach are unusual because, in their position, nothing would stop me laughing.

There was a third occasion when I was walking down a path with my father's dachshund trotting behind me. It had been raining and the concrete paving stones were wet. I was wearing a pair of washable plastic shoes, which proved not to have the desired surface holding ability.

All of a sudden, I felt my feet slide out from under me and the ballet begin. After a suitable dance, I collapsed on my back into red mud with my limbs in spaghetti mode. Kaiser, the dog, thinking I was playing some new game for his entertainment, jumped all over my front with his muddy paws.

My friend, Frances, who was backing her car down the drive at the time, leaned on her window and laughed her fill. Nobody else laughed except the pair of us.

Eventually, the trusty domestic worker, without a smile, came and helped me up, so I could go inside and change my clothes and shower.

Unicyclists and Pianos

I had a very important job on the stage show I was working on. During a four second blackout, I had to throw back the curtain closing the proscenium arch to allow a unicyclist to cycle through and be on the stage cycling around when the lights came up.

One night I threw back the curtain and the unicyclist did not pass through. She had fallen over onto me and I was spread-eagled and pinned against the side of the doorway. In the excitement of the moment, it took a couple of seconds for the situation to filter through to my brain.

As soon as I realised what had happened, I grabbed the wrist of the arm closest to the unicycle and rider and swung my arm, flinging them off me, rather too violently, because they hit the other side of the doorway. I only had one thing on my mind and that was to get them onto the stage before the lights came up. I ran behind, righted the unicycle and gave an almighty push. Both unicycle combination and the light came on at the same time.

When the crisis was over, I realised that some time in the process my neck had been put out. It was so uncomfortable, that after a couple of days, I made an appointment with a chiropractor.

When I entered the chiropractor's office, he was sitting behind his desk with my file in front of him, pen poised to take notes.

"What is the problem?" he asked.

"My neck is out," I replied.

"How did it happen?" he droned.

"A unicyclist fell on me," I supplied.

The chiropractor looked at me, carefully placed his pen on the desk, parallel with the top of the file, and folded his hands over the top of the notes. "I think you had better tell me the whole story," he drawled.

I proceeded to explain how the situation came about with appropriate actions. When I got to the part where I had elbowed the unicycle off me, I got my thumb caught in the string of beads I was wearing and the string broke, sending a shower of bead up into the air. Beads came down like rainfall pretty uniformly over the whole office, bouncing off furniture and our heads and shoulders before rolling into their final resting places. Somehow, a significant number went down the nose hole in the adjustable couch and lodged themselves in the cogs beneath.

There was another person able to keep a completely straight face during what, to me, was a hilarious situation. It was difficult for me to contain myself but I tried. I think I am beginning to understand what happens – people who aren't used to bizarre situations just cannot believe what they are seeing.

After the chiropractor had repositioned my bones with alarming cracking sounds, we ended the session with both of us crawling around the office floor retrieving beads and flicking them out of the cogs with pens.

As I walked down the drive on my way out to my car, I heard the chiropractor start to sing at the top of his voice. I have no idea what the significance of that was.

Some years later, we were moving an upright piano for parents' night. One of the transporters lost their footing and the piano started to topple. For some strange reason, I thought I could save it and rushed to its rescue, but it was bigger and heavier than I was.

It fell over trapping me beneath it, leaving me with a scrape down my left shin which ended in a dent.

All the staff rushed up. The piano was lifted off and I sat up. The pain was excruciating. Sweat ran down my face. I did not know what to do with myself. I felt faint, so I lay back. Once down there, I felt nauseous so I sat up. I did sit ups for some time while the wide-eyed staff stood around me staring. They had just completed a first aid course and had learnt that patients who are silent are often the ones who are most badly injured.

Eventually, they decided to carry me into my bedroom and place me on the bed. Someone got a tea towel full of ice to place on the contusion. They phoned Ted, who told them to give me a painkiller.

The painkiller kicked in quite quickly and I started to think about the last time something unusual had fallen on me – the unicyclist. I began to laugh. That made the staff look even more worried and once again they stood around me staring. This made me laugh even more.

A Pleasant Lunch with Friends

We have a delightful friend, who is an amazing cook and loves to show hospitality to her friends by inviting them round once or twice a year for a lunch party. She then produces course after course of delicious Indian cuisine.

The parties are usually held out in the garden and a lot of the cooking takes place in the nearby outdoor kitchen.

The table is always decorated with colourful lengths of cloth, artistic ceramic crockery and ceramic "glasses".

Anita has a special friend who comes from London every year for a visit. They are two of a kind, and know each other's ways of thinking.

On this particular day, Anita was busy preparing food (each course arrives straight from the fire onto your plate) and her London friend was laying the table when we arrived. Everyone set to, doing what they could to help and getting acquainted (Anita's friends are diverse and there were always new combinations at every gathering). When we had finished, we sat down to chat and sip wine.

One of the ladies had a sewing bag with her and was busy tacking bits of material together. She explained to us that she was due to fly overseas for her son's wedding in a few days and was making a two piece suit for the occasion. She went on to say what difficulty she was having finding the right material to make a blouse to go with the skirt and jacket. Just then, she placed the article of clothing she was sewing on the table. Everybody's eyes were drawn to the same spot, because everyone could see that the cloth on the table was the PERFECT match. Nobody said anything until Anita's friend broke the silence with the words, "Clear the table. I'm going to get a pair of scissors."

"But, but …" said the tailor lady.

"Oh, Anita won't mind," said the friend. "She will be happy."

In no time at all, we had taken everything off the piece of cloth which was doing duty as a tablecloth. It had been doubled over and then folded back some – there was plenty of it. The more we looked at it, the better we could all see that there would never be a better combination.

"But, but …" said the tailor lady.

"How much do you need?" interrupted Anita's friend wielding a large pair of scissors.

"About two and a half meters, but . . ." stammered the lady.

"Right!" said Anita's friend. We all stepped forward to help measure out the required amount.

In a short time the required length of material had been separated from the tablecloth, folded and stowed in the sewing bag.

We were just finishing off the resetting of the table, when Anita appeared with the first course. Her friend explained what we had been up to.

Just as her friend had predicted, Anita was delighted that she was able to provide the material to finish off the outfit and even offered her extra material and found a scarf which added a chic touch.

Taking a Tram Ride

I was on a six week holiday with two girl friends in America. My American friend had invited us and we had been planning the trip for a year.

As per "the best laid plans of mice and men" adage, things had not followed the expected schedule. By the date we were due to move house, the money transfer had not gone through and the old lady we were purchasing the house from (quite understandably) would not move out and let us move in, until the money was in her bank. However, (less understandably) even after the transfer went through, the lady still delayed.

Consequently, we ended up moving the day before I was due to fly out. The movers had been ordered for the morning but they did not arrive until late afternoon and it was after 8pm when they carried the last of the furniture into the new house.

Needless to say, the time between then and when I had to leave for the airport the next afternoon, were filled with me madly rushing about trying to make the place look as homely as possible. In order to make things easier, I had not emptied any drawers. I had just piled them into my car and we slid them into the appropriate furniture as soon as it was in place. I had a suitcase under my bed and had been throwing things for the trip into it for the past month.

We had to make a U-turn on our way to the airport because I had left my passport at home, or thought I had. We made another U-turn shortly afterwards when I found the passport tucked between other papers. I dropped my air ticket in the airport, but thankfully was soon reunited with it.

Once we, finally, took off and were on our way, I relaxed back in my seat. That only lasted for a minute. I dived into my handbag and my worst fears were confirmed. I had forgotten to bank my husband's pay cheque.

All the worst case scenarios ran through my mind. "The family would not be able to pay the bond repayments on the house, and we would be homeless!" was the most alarming. Eventually, sense prevailed and I decided I would phone the family from Lisbon airport during the stop over, and they could get the cheque cancelled and replaced with a new one. I felt more relaxed after that decision but not enough to sleep. Apart from anything, I am terrible at remembering numbers and I was not sure that the phone number I had in my head for the house was correct.

Once in Lisbon airport, I left my friends relaxing in a lounge we had found, enquired about the code for Zimbabwe and attempted to phone – for the next two hours.

I was becoming more and more agitated. Then the man who gave me the codes beckoned me over and apologised, confessing that he had given me the wrong codes.

Amazingly, I got straight through after that. Once I had sorted the money issue out, I could give myself up to enjoying the trip.

Whatever happened, I was determined to enjoy it. It was tough at times. My American friend is dyslexic and it showed.

She lost my friend, Phyllis, and I in Washington DC quite early on in the trip, due to giving us an incorrect address to meet her at, after she returned the hire car.

We walked about 20 blocks and were still lost at 8pm at night. Luckily, we had dropped our luggage off at the home we were staying at and remembered the name of a major road. If we could get on the road, we were fairly sure that we would be able to find our way to the house.

We climbed into a taxi. The driver, who reminded me of a TV star, was not happy, when we were not sure where we wanted to go. However, between us we managed to find the house.

We sat on the front lawn of the house while our friends scoured the city looking for us. Finally, they phoned a neighbour to check if we had turned up and we were reunited.

You cannot go to San Francisco and not experience a tram ride, and our American friend wanted us to experience everything possible. (Even to the extent of wishing for an earthquake around point 4 on the Richter scale – which annoyed her mother because they had one in the area of her house, and we were not there. "Trust Helen," said her mother. "She orders these things and then she isn't here to receive them!")

We drove round, and round and round – well more like up and down – in San Francisco trying to make our way to the plaza from which the trams started off. There were endless one way streets and we always seemed to be on roads going in the opposite direction to the way we wanted to go.

Finally, we reached the area around Nob Hill, on top of which perched the famous Waldorf Astoria Hotel. At this point, we began to be passed by a succession of emergency vehicles with lights flashing and sirens blaring – a police car, a fire engine, another police car, an ambulance and so on.

"Well," said Helen, "I am glad we are not going wherever they are going."

When we reached the tram station, the only parking we could find, had 15 minute parking meters. After going around a couple of times, Helen decided that we were going to park there anyway.

From the car, we crossed to an island and then to the plaza. There was no ticket booth; you had to do battle with a vending machine. The machine was very particular about the money it accepted. It had to be the right way up, correct side, have no turned corners, be properly aligned etc.

After many attempts we managed to get three tickets to take us to the end of the run and back. We looked about and saw a line of trolley cars standing, but no staff members were visible. We chose seats on the front trolley and sat down to wait.

Nearby, squatting on a bench was a man. We presumed he was a homeless man. He kept sticking his right arm in the air and shouting out some sort of gibberish as he waved his hand down. Every now and again, we heard him say something which we could understand like: "How ya, Fred?" or "Got a cigarette, Mike?" Then he would be off with gibberish and gesticulating again.

Phyllis, who was subject to agitation, became agitated. "It's cold. Helen, you need a jersey. What is that man saying? He is driving me crazy! The meter is going to expire. We are going to get a ticket."

Eventually, Helen decided to go across to the car, put more money into the meter and get a jersey. She crossed over to the island, reached the car, fed the meter, got the jersey and was on her way back. She had reached the island when the trolley started to pull away. We had been so busy watching her we had not noticed that a driver and conductor had arrived. Phyllis and I, with the experience of been lost in a big city still fresh in our minds, catapulted off the tram. We were not going to let Helen out of our sights.

When Helen reached us we started the process all over again, seating ourselves in the next trolley. Peace prevailed for a while as we chattered. The man continued his antics.

As the minutes ticked by Phyllis became agitated just as before. "What's he saying? What's he saying? It's driving me mad! The meter's going to expire. We are going to get a parking ticket." Eventually, she decided to go and put money in the meter.

Phyllis, trotted off onto the island, reached the car, put money in the meter and was on the island on her way back, when the trolley started to pull off. Helen and I jumped off.

We seated ourselves in the next trolley. The man continued his strange and incomprehensible actions.

Phyllis soon became agitated again. "What's he saying? What's he saying? It's driving me mad! The meter's going to expire. We are going to get a parking ticket." Eventually, she decided it was my turn to go and put money in the meter.

Off I went, over the island, put money into the meter and as I stepped onto the island, the trolley started to move. Helen and Phyllis jumped off.

Helen lost patience. "Right," she said firmly, "I do not care if we get a ticket. We are not getting off this trolley!"

We stoically sat through the cries of the man squatting on the bench and Phyllis's agitation.

Finally, a huge man and a tiny woman entered the tram. The huge man began to check our tickets and the tiny woman threw herself into an enormous lever in the middle of the tram, which was almost as tall as she was. It seemed that she, not the large man, was the tram operator. It looked most incongruous.

The tram trundled up Nob Hill. As we passed right by the Waldorf Astoria Hotel we had a good close up view of all the emergency vehicles we had seen before – they were parked all round it. At each entrance was a policeman, his back against the wall, holding a drawn gun - so much for not going where they were going.

We ran to the end of the line – I hardly noticed anything of the passing scenery, so entranced was I by what was going on at the hotel.

On the way back, the situation remained the same round the hotel. It was like living in a film – a strange dreamlike feeling stole over me.

Back at the plaza, the man was still crying forth. We did not have a parking ticket.

That night at our motel, after the fright Helen gave us by secretly dropping money in a slot which caused the beds to vibrate, we switched on the news. The beds were massage beds, designed to relax us, but they had the opposite effect because we thought we were experiencing one of the earthquakes Helen had wished on us.

We learned that some weeks before, the Waldorf Astoria had been set on fire by an arsonist. On her rounds, a chambermaid had come across the very same man. She had screamed and thrown the sheets she was carrying into the air and run to raise the alarm.

A 911 call had resulted in the mass arrival of all the emergency vehicles we had witnessed. The police sealed off all the entrances and if you were in you had to remain in, and if you were out you could not get in. They then did a room by room search. They did not manage to find the arsonist, but two policemen shot each other in the excitement.

Rebecca Viljoen

The Buzz

One Saturday morning, I surfaced from a deep sleep, with a dull buzzing sound in my ears. Naturally, I tried to ignore it and go back to sleep, but it persisted until I was completely awake. Lying on my back, I tried to understand its significance. Finally, I had to resign myself to getting up to investigate.

I wandered about testing the volume until I located the source. There were thousands of bees buzzing around a plastic bowl on the verandah. These were African bees – the undiluted, more potent version of KILLER BEES.

Then, it came back to me. The previous night, I had returned home and stepped out of the car into a plastic bowl. I had picked up the bowl and taken it into the light of the kitchen. There I had discovered that it was full of honey comb – and bees, so I had taken it and left it on the front verandah to deal with in the morning. Unfortunately, the neighbourhood bees were earlier risers than I was and they were busily engaged in collecting the honey and removing it to their various hives as fast as they could.

We had had to ask a gardener to leave our employ a few weeks before. Whether by accident or design, he had his revenge by leaving a swarm of bees in a homemade hive in some long grass at the back of the property. The bees were very cranky and came roaring out and made their displeasure known in no uncertain terms, every time the new gardener attempted to cut the grass.

The new gardener did not seem overly concerned about being stung, but Louis was allergic to bees and May become more and more concerned after every attack. She decided to do something, and phoned a bee remover.

The bee remover made an appointment to come when it was getting dark. He smoked the bees and removed them. My elder son, feeling that it was unfair that he be paid, got a swarm of bees and honey, prevailed upon him to leave honey in the bowl provided.

The irony was that the bee problem, which had been 300 meters away, was now practically in the house.

As nobody else seemed to be going to do anything but look at the bees through the closed windows, I decided I had better step into the gap. Louis, who had a lively interest both in the activities of the bees and the honey comb, of which he was particularly fond, persisted in getting as close as possible to the action. My husband, Ted, at regular intervals, lead Louis away from the vicinity and closed all the inter-leading doors, in a vain attempt to confine him as far away as possible.

I decided that my best plan of action was to close the honey cone in plastic icecream containers. In order to protect myself as best as possible, I dressed in a thick track suit and put long, thick socks on both my hands and feet. My sturdiest shoes were running shoes, so I chose the hardiest pair. To complete the ensemble, I placed a large straw hat on my head, and topped it with a mosquito net. Ted said I looked like the bride of Dracula.

It took a bit of practice to move within the mosquito net. At first I had a tendency to walk up the side of it so that after a few steps I was bent over with my head centimeters from my feet. Eventually, I discovered that if I kicked the mosquito net in front of me with a sweeping step,

I could progress quite well. It was a movement half way between a bridal march and a goose step.

Armed with five or six containers, I stepped out onto the verandah and heard the door close firmly behind me. I put the containers down and picked up the plastic bowl and carried it into the middle of the lawn. The bees rose up peevishly and buzzed threateningly. Leaving the bowl on the lawn I went back for the containers.

Quickly, I transferred honey cone into the containers and closed the lids firmly. When the last bit was firmly sealed in, I took the bowl and rinsed it out.

The bees had been protesting regularly, by synchronizing their buzzing and doing formation flying, in a menacing manner. This was quite disturbing, and I felt my heart reply by thumping loudly whenever they did it. The odd bee found its way inside the net, at which point, I had to stop what I was doing while I madly tried to prevent it from discharging its sting into my exposed skin. It probably looked like Dracula's bride doing the monster mash at double speed. When there was no more honey in the bowl, I thought that the bees would go on their way, but I was wrong. They opted for a sit in – on top of my head.

I spent twenty minutes trying various manoeuvres in an attempt to dislodge the bees. My family watched the spectacle through the closed windows. Though the bees occasionally rose in their synchronised – and intimidating protests, they almost immediately settled back on top of my head.

Reluctantly, I signed to my family that, I required fly spray. I do not like to kill bees and I do not like insecticides, and I definitely do not like to spray myself with poison. A can of fly spray was thrown out of a hastily opened and closed window.

I sprayed around my head and, fortunately, the bees gave up pretty soon and most of them went on their way - and I was allowed back inside the house.

I was lucky to have escaped with only a few stings. If I was expecting any recognition or admiration of the way I handled the crisis, I was sadly disappointed. My family all went back to what they had been doing now the entertainment was over, and I was left to divest myself of my costume and take a bath and wash my hair.

A Toilet Break

At the engineering company where I worked, the ladies' toilet was located inside the workshop. As long as the weather was good, we walked around the outside of the building and in through the back door. Once inside the toilet, we always locked ourselves securely in.

One day, when I wanted to leave the toilet, I turned the key and tried to leave but the door would not budge. I turned the key again and tried the door, with the same result. Removing the key, I discovered that the end had broken off and I only had the stem.

In the workshop, there was a constant cacophony of busy machines, lathes, punches, drills etc. No amount of knocking on the door would be heard. I went to the window, and was just able to see the workman at the machine inside the back door. I am not a good whistler at the best of times and I was overcome by a case of the giggles, which further hampered my attempts.

Eventually, I managed to attract the man's attention. He came over to the window, but he was unable to speak English. After failing to understand my problem, he suddenly turned on his heel and walked off. I was a little taken back; perhaps I was in for the long term.

To my relief, the worker returned soon after with the office cleaner / tea maker. I explained the problem and Peter listened and went off without comment. The worker went back to his machine. Getting used to the abrupt departures, I awaited developments.

Sure enough, in a short while, Peter returned with my office colleague, Mandy. Mandy's first reaction was to laugh until she had to lean on the wall. When she had pulled herself together sufficiently, she and Peter walked off.

I waited expectantly, but nobody seemed to be coming. I was getting bored – there is only so much you can do in a rest room. Trying to see what was happening in the outside world, I peered through the keyhole – straight into the eye of my boss, who was looking in from the workshop side. I got quite a fright and started back. When I cautiously looked again, the eye had changed – my boss had enlisted the assistance of the workshop manager.

When they drew back, I could see them discussing the best course of action but all I could hear was the clatter of machinery.

My mind wandered to my friend's young daughter. She had locked herself in her aunt's third floor flat bathroom once. My friend's husband called the fire brigade and asked for a long ladder.

Inexplicably, the firemen knocked on the door of the flat and, before the occupants could say anything, rushed through the flat and hacked the bathroom door down with their hatchets.

It did have the beneficial effect of frightening the little girl out of the locking spree she had been on.

Nothing dramatic happened in my case, unless you consider nearly dying of boredom during the half an hour it took to dismantle the lock to the point where it no longer held the door closed.

The Day I Thought the World Had Come to an End

I do not know if you have ever been in a situation where you are unable to make any sense of what is going on. If you have, you will understand the complete feeling of disorientation it engenders and how your boggled mind grabs onto any idea, however bizarre, in its attempt to find something familiar or some acceptable explanation for the events presented to it.

The first time it happened to me was the result of answering the ringing land line phone.

The lady on the other end of the line did not identify herself and immediately launched into a long involved story.

"We move houses. We have rented out the house. The people who are renting are horrible people. My daughter and granddaughter and one son are moving to South Africa. My other son has not decided what he wants to do yet, but we cannot afford to keep up the house..." said the voice.

My mind soon split itself into two, half trying to follow the story and the other half desperately trying to identify the speaker and find some link between the person and/or the situation they were describing, and me. Failing on all accounts, my mind swirled about in utter confusion finding no anchor or reference point.

"... I am staying with my mother. The others are with my brother. We have rented the house to some people. They are horrible people. We have had to leave our three cats ... " the woman continued.

I suppose I could have asked her who she was, but I have difficulty remembering the names of people and I am used to giving myself time for things to fall into place. Besides, there had not yet been a break in the story big enough for me to interject into. Things were not falling into place in this instance, and my mind was becoming dizzy. It started to wander.

It was a bit like the time I was asked to make a plan drawing of a plant room. I stood looking at different sized pipes and air conditioning ducts coming into or going out of every wall and the floor and ceiling, sometimes running together for short distances, separating and going in new directions, flowing under and over each other, suddenly diving through the floor or soaring through the ceiling - like some kind of six dimensional spaghetti junction. Suddenly, I fell over. I'd lost my reference point and was not able to orientate myself as to what was up, down or horizontal.

"... so Greta said ..." she continued.

My mind skidded to a halt. It had heard something it was familiar with. My best friend was called Greta. "Greta! Greta!" said my mind, hugging the word, every bit as relieved as if I had been wandering lost for days in a forest and had suddenly seen someone I knew coming to my rescue. Mentally I flipped through the people I knew associated with Greta. Happily, I zoomed in. The lady on the line must be Greta's mother! I did not really know her, but I had met her.

After that, things were still a little unusual, but not befuddling. It turned out that my friend's mother (a person I barely knew) wanted me to go to the house she owned (to which I had never been) and had rented out to horrible people, and capture three cats (which I had never seen and would consider me a stranger) that they had had to leave behind, and take them to the SPCA.

This was a bit of a tall order but, compared to what I had just experienced, seemed almost normal.

The situation continued to be surreal because, when I got to the house, the back garden was completely filled with huge sunflowers which towered overhead. As I threaded my way between the giant flowers armed with plates of cat food, calling, "Sxxxxsxxxxx," I wondered if this was how Alice felt after she ate the mushroom and shrank. Alice's adventures were not real, but then my adventure did not seem real either, and I had not even eaten any mushrooms.

It is probably that unsure feeling which keeps people from trying unfamiliar things. It isn't comfortable, but adventures do make life interesting, for me anyway. To add to the strangeness, was a feeling of getting taller and heavier. This was because the soil was damp and clay and, with each step I took, another layer of it attached itself to the bottom of my shoes.

I did, to my surprise manage to capture two of the cats, but the third evaded me even after a second visit.

The second time I became disorientated was when a friend rang me in the middle of the night and asked for my help in rescuing her daughter, whose car had broken down.

I was unable to rouse my husband or either of my sons. Eventually, feeling that time was of the essence, I let myself out of the house and garden and drove off to the rescue.

As I drove towards my friend's place, I was not sure if I was dreaming or not and imagined that I might be sleep driving (a type of vehicularly assisted sleep walking). I imagined explaining to my friend why I was at her front gate at 2am – if I was dreaming. However, the thought of her daughter possibly being in danger egged me on to be sure.

As it turned out, I had not been dreaming and we spent the next few hours driving around trying to find the girl and her friend. We did not have cell phones yet and only had a vague idea of where to look.

Luckily, all was resolved happily in the end. I went back to bed, and nobody even notice that I had been out.

The most disturbing incident of all took place in the flat we rented. It was on the first floor. There was no security for laundry downstairs, so I used to hang our washing on clothes horses placed on the balcony of our flat.

I was sitting on the end of the bed one day, when a movement caught my eye, and I looked up. As I watched, all four paws of our cat came slowly down from behind a tea towel and then slowly rose up again. Watching the repeated slow, graceful levitating and lowering of the four pinky-ginger paws, alarm filled me. My mind said that what it was seeing was impossible, and its immediate explanation was that the world had come to an end and all the natural laws had been abolished.

My heart began to race and the alarm in me rose to a higher level with each appearance and disappearance taking place before my eyes. My instinct was to run but, taking myself in hand and gathering all my courage, I fearfully forced myself to approach the clothes horse. Time seemed to have slowed down, and I felt as if I was making my way through air as thick as treacle. I battled to draw air into my lungs.

Rebecca Viljoen

As soon as I got close enough, I snatched at the tea towel and pulled it off the clothes horse. . .

I stood for some seconds digesting what had been revealed. Seemingly unconcerned and even to be enjoying the gentle movement caused by the expanding and contracting of the elastic, the cat lay across a bra I had fastened over one of the bars of the clothes horse. The cat had somehow settled itself along the loop, with its paws hanging down each side. I am not sure how it was managing to make the elastic do what it was doing. It might have been the rhythm of its breathing.

There ARE Angels

My friend, Frances, has had a succession of motor vehicles which almost defy description in their quirks and mechanical short comings. One of these amazing vehicles used to sip its fuel from a bowl on the front passenger side floor. I should have known better than to agree to venture to be transported by one of them, but times were hard and I had to give Frances a chance to share.

A friend of ours lived in a large retirement village, and they were holding a Burn's Night celebration in their community centre. Furthermore, our friend was to play her piano accordion in the dance band, and we were urged to come and support her.

On the due date, quite unsuspecting, I sat down in the passenger seat of Frances's vehicle and relaxed back. In the wink of an eye, I found myself upside down on the back seat. The passenger seat was not anchored to the floor, in the usual manner, or in any manner at all, and it had somersaulted me effortlessly through the air with a single buck. In addition, there were no seat belts.

Having extracted myself from the back, I, eventually, managed to get myself into a position on the front seat which felt fairly stable. One hand firmly grasped the arm rest on the door, the other hand was braced against the cubbyhole, one foot was braced against the side of the front well and the other was dug into the floor of the well.

Rebecca Viljoen

Before we even left the yard, I was having misgivings about the ability of the vehicle to deliver us to our destination. There appeared to be a little man in the engine with a hammer, and the engine did not run any too smoothly. I asked Frances nervously if she was sure we shouldn't take my car. She shrugged off with disdain my nervousness, and my suggestion.

My anxiety increased before we had gone two blocks because, as well as the obvious problems, it became apparent that there were other hidden defects. Each time we hit a bump, and there were many bumps, either the lights, engine or both stopped functioning until we hit the next bump. My eyes wide with horror, I reiterated more urgently that we had better go back and fetch my car. Frances was just as adamant that it was unnecessary. I gripped more tightly onto my anchor points.

We had not gone much farther when the whole car began to fill up with smoke, originating from a grey metal, lumpy thing situated under the dashboard, which had many different coloured wires running into and out of it. That was too much. I tried to be firm about going back and getting my car. Frances turned a deaf ear, wound her window down and stepped on the gas. I had no option but to hang on, and try not to look.

To my surprise, we did actually make it to the venue of the Burn's Night celebration, where further surprises awaited us. I spent over half an hour gazing at the band, which consisted entirely of old ladies – I think. The pianist had the appearance of being kept up well beyond her bedtime and in danger of nodding off at any moment. Both the electric guitarist and drummer were dressed in men's suits - I was not sure if they were men, or women in drag, or vice versa. Our friend was the only ordinary looking person in the set, and we knew her to be quite unusual in her own way.

We ate haggis and potatoes and had a meagre slice of slightly burnt jam tart. Frances was irritated because there was no coffee though, to be in the character of the meal, tea was probably more in keeping – or whisky.

All too soon, it was time to start on our perilous journey home and I anchored myself in preparation.

All went well, until we reached a major intersection about a kilometer or so from home. We had drawn into the middle of the road in order to turn, and the engine stopped and refused to start.

It was the middle of the night but, for some unknown reason, there was heavy traffic. I asked Frances if I should get out and push.

"Yes", she said, so I got out. "No," she contradicted, so I got back in.

For what seemed an interminable time, Frances yesed and noed and I hopped in and out, alternating with matadorlike sweeps of the door, in order to avoid the charges of passing cars. Eventually, the car deigned to start and we lurched on our way.

The last stretch of road before home was very dark with no street lighting. The car hit a bump and the lights went out, and stayed out.

That was the last straw and I became hysterical, gripping and pushing more strongly into my anchor position and crying, "I cannot see where we are going! Can you see where we are going?!"

Frances ignored me and put her foot down. It reminded me of Space Mountain in Disney Land – a roller coaster in the dark.

When we stopped at home, I was so tensed up that I had difficulty straightening out of my bracing stance. I felt like a butterfly emerging from its chrysalis.

To my alarm, Ted offered Frances coffee, which she gladly accepted. It was midnight and I had suffered trauma – I wanted to unwind. Coffee! I needed brandy! I smiled, hid my chagrin and played the gracious hostess.

Frances happily drank coffee, and the cat settled herself comfortably on Frances's lap.

After what seemed like days, Frances was finally ready to leave. There was a slight tussle as we unhooked the cat from Frances's legs. The disgruntled cat had intended to sleep until dawn, and dug her claws in deep, in an attempt to hold down the snug bed which was intent on walking away.

The car had decided that it had done enough for one night. Nothing would persuade it to start its engine. For all I knew, the little man was probably what kept the engine alive and he had sensibly gone to bed. I could imagine him beating the engine into working, like the man with the whip beating the rowers in the Viking ships. Anyway, Ted had to drive Frances home.

The next morning, I was curious about the lumpy thing under the dashboard of Frances's car which had filled the car with smoke. Interestingly enough, there had not been any smoke in the car on the way home. I found that the only way I could get a good view of it was to sling my legs over the back of the seat and stick my head under the dash board. Sure enough, there was a wire floating around loose. I stuck it into a spare hole. I was rewarded with a shower of sparks on my face, and the car started.

Oh, my hat! I was going through the gate again, was what flashed through my mind – with my feet over the back of the seat and my head under the dash!

Flashback

*A couple of years previously, I had borrowed my son's car to go to work.
His car had a grey lumpy thing under the dash too. On the way home from
work, the car stopped, and stubbornly refused all efforts to start it again.
I went into a nearby factory to phone my family for help, but nobody was
at home.*

*The helpful receptionist offered to see if there was anyone in the workshop
who could help. I accepted her offer gratefully.*

*Who came to my aid was not one, but five very small men – really small
men. I felt like Snow White.*

*Anyway, the men swarmed around the car, identified the lumpy thing as
the source of the proble,m and got the car started. They brushed off my
profuse thanks, and told me what to do if the car stopped again.*

*It was the rush hour and I negotiated the traffic, expecting the car to stop
again at any time.*

*When I reached home, I was so relieved that I made the mistake of trying
to get out and open the gate with the car in gear. The door was open and I
had one leg stuck out, when the seat hit me in the back and the car began
to buck towards the gate. I gripped onto the steering wheel, while my leg
described circles, like I was on a bucking bronco. We crashed through the
gate, and we were lurching towards the neighbour's fence before I had
enough presence of mind to switch off the engine.*

*A friend, who happened to be walking up the drive at the time, rushed up
to me, with her eyes wide in fright, and asked me if I was all right.*

Very quickly, I removed the wire. I was in no position to be in control of a car, and I had no desire to destroy a second gate, or bear panel beating costs.

Whatever, I believe that there are guardian angels. There is no other way to explain how Frances remains alive while driving about in such contraptions.

Mark's Week

Our son, Mark, had a job with a computer company doing networking. At the beginning of the week he had been working on the computers in a private club situated in an old house, which must have been one of the oldest houses in the city. His assistant and he were working in a large room with a bar. At the bar, were two people enjoying a peaceful drink. Nobody else was in the whole room. Mark's assistant was up in the ceiling running some cables. All of a sudden, the assistant fell through the ceiling right above the two people at the bar, who were instantly covered from head to foot in a fine black dust, which must have been accumulating in the ceiling for about a hundred years.

Later that week, I entered the kitchen to find Mark downing glass after glass of water. That was a sure sign that he had had a shock.

When he had recovered sufficiently, he recounted how he had been on his way home on the double carriageway. A pickup truck going in the opposite direction, on the other side of the carriageway, had hit the curb. Travelling in the back of the truck was a man and a mattress. The shock caused by the bump had catapulted both the man and the mattress out of the truck, into the air and across to Mark's side of the street.

The mattress landed on the road in front of him, and the man, unpredictably and coincidentally but fortunately, landed on the mattress. Seeing Mark bearing down on him, with remarkable presence of mind, the man had leapt up, grabbed the mattress and run to the side of the road, a split second before Mark hit him.

What a week!

Another One of Those Weeks

We were due to fly out to visit our sons in Australia that week. My car battery died. The generator battery had died a couple of months previously, and we had been pull-starting it since then. My car did not allow for that option.

The previous Thursday had been windy, and the bamboos had broken three of the four power lines which supply us three phase electricity. Strangely, nearly all of our lights and three plugs were working. The neighbours had everything out. The borehole was out, so we did not have water unless we used the generator.

Neither Ted nor I could find the visas I had printed out (the visa papers never did resurface) and Ted had also lost his blood test paper. I spent ages looking for the papers. I found Ted's blood test papers among the rubbish in his car.

I went to reprint our visas and found that the surge protector had blown in the office (courtesy of the bamboos). I changed the surge protector and printed new visas. Then, I ran a cable, from the pantry, into the kitchen to connect the fridge, and one through the whole house to connect the TV. The house looked like it had become infested by some large variety of worm. I was constantly getting tangled up in the cable, and in danger of disconnecting everything.

Early Friday morning, I was dozing because I had had one of those nights where you feel awake all night. Ted rushed in, turned on the light, and announced that the generator was broken. He had been trying to pull start it to pump up some water, and the pull cable had broken. I blearily dragged myself out of bed and got half dressed in order to help.

Ted was normally at work when we needed the generator, so I was more familiar with its quirks. I noticed that the fuel switch was off. The generator had been serviced and the fuel switch had not been switched back on.

We put a new rope pull on, but that broke after a couple of pulls, so we began again using nylon washing line and, eventually, got the generator started. Ted switched on the borehole and the generator coughed and stopped. The fuel switch was off again. This time nothing we did worked and we could not get it started, so there was no water and thirty people needing to use toilets.

Ted went off to get a battery for the generator, in case that would make a difference, but it did not.

We called an electrician to come and move the borehole onto the working circuit, and a mechanic, because I suspected that the problem with the generator was fuel starvation. The electrician was busy on a job. Luckily, the mechanic was in the area. He came but he had no tools, and finding tools is a mission round here because Ted works on a NTSPT (Never Tools in Same Place Twice) system.

It took the mechanic about two hours to find the problem. The eco fuel (blend) that we are forced to use had made the rubber end of the pin in the needle and seat swell, which stopped the flow of fuel. In the meantime, luckily, it had rained and there was some water in the barrel to flush toilets with.

At 10am there was no water for tea, but the tap by the chicken run suddenly had some water - it was really odd. There was no water in any of the other taps.

Anyway, the mechanic had the generator running before the electrician was free, so we cancelled him. That turned out to be a good thing too because, if he had connected the borehole, everything could have blown up, as it should not have been working in the first place.

One of the teachers was off sick, and I was supposed to sit in her class, but I only managed about ten minutes the whole morning. I missed one of my special reading tuitions too.

The next day, the electricity people came to repair the wires. That is when I discovered what a jungle the gardener had allowed to propagate back there. The electricity people told us that we had to pay liability - repair and materials for the lines, labour for three people, transport and the fuse blown at the substation. However, they would be open for a bribe. Usually, I take my medicine and take responsibility, but I did not have that kind of money. Add a bad conscience to my other stresses.

I was great to have lights in the lounge, and to get rid of all the flex running through the house, but then we discovered that the hot water heater had been blown, so we had to call the electrician in on Monday, and continue with cold water washes.

The very weird thing was the electricity continuing on one line. It must have been going to earth, and we were meant to be getting shocks. One of the electricity technicians said it was the first time in twenty years on the job that he had seen such a thing.

Then there was the water which had appeared in the tap at tea time. It was a tap right in the middle of the garden. Never had to happened before or since, and we do not know where it could have come from. Our municipal water had been cut off six years before, due to an administrative error, and we had stopped paying the bills. We were still writing occasional letters about it.

I felt special. It made up a great deal for all the inconveniences.

Ek Non Comprondero

I have the usual problems with cell phones – they get stolen or lost. I lost one in my garden, when nobody else but Ted and I were home - never found it. One of my cells had an annoying habit of saying it was "busy" when I tried to access my contacts. Short of living a life of its own, how can a phone be "busy" when you want to look at the list of people you have phone numbers for, for goodness sake?!

When we arrived in Melbourne, after travelling for about twenty-four hours – there was not anyone to meet us at the airport, as there had been a misunderstanding. Ted and I walked out to the pickup area (which involved crossing three zebra crossings – the one closest to the terminal had a lollipop man). Heaven knows what that man thought, because I went over his crossing about twelve times in the next hour. I went back to the airport terminal building to buy a sim card for my phone, leaving Ted guarding the luggage in the pick-up zone.

The lady in the shop was very helpful – no problem - $30. She said I could use her phone while she put the new sim card into mine. I had left the number of my friend in the baggage with Ted, so I had to go back and fetch it.

Back at the shop, I made the phone call on the shop phone. My friend thought our younger son was going to pick us up. She undertook to phone him and get him to the airport, as he was closest. The shop assistant handed me my phone and said everything was good to go.

I trotted back to Ted. However, when I tapped in my son's number, the screen filled with icons and a bunch of words I could not understand.

I trotted back to the shop. The lady was under the impression that the language on the phone was my home language. I exclaimed that it certainly was not – I spoke English. She said that was very strange, she had never had such a thing happen before. She turned to the computer to try and find out what language it was, all the time exclaiming how strange it all was. I told her not to worry, as things like this happened to me often.

After about ten minutes of tapping away she exclaimed, "No way! All these words come from a different language!"

While she was doing battle with my phone, the shop phone rang. It was my friend. My son and his partner had had an alcoholic beverage, so they could not pick us up. Australia is very strict about such things. She was coming.

Eventually, the shop assistant discovered that the language was Lunfado. It took around half an hour to sort out the phone, while she kept exclaiming how she had never come across anything like it happening before.

I got back to Ted and phoned our son. He said that he was on his way to fetch us in a taxi - could we go to the top of the terminus.

We crossed the many crossings and passed the lollipop man. In the building we were told the top was for drop off only, and there was a hefty fine for being picked up there.

I phoned our son, and we went back past the lollipop man, and back to our original position, where we were, eventually, reunited with our son after fourteen years.

We looked up Lunfardo on the internet the next day (when we finally surfaced about 12pm Australian time – 8am Africa time). One site said that it was a slang language made up of German, Italian and Spanish by the Nazi German and Fascist Italian people who immigrated to Spanish speaking Argentina, after the II World War – that seemed to be the version that had appeared on my phone.

Another site said it was a prison slang spoken by criminals and is now associated with the slang language spoken in an area of Buenos Aires!

Not only is it strange that a different language came onto my phone, but it is **slang** spoken by **criminals** in one city in the world and so it is not actually even a language. Nobody I have spoken to has heard of Lunfardo, and neither would I have if this had not happened.

See, I Am Not Making Them Up

Just recently, my guardian angel has been kind enough to arrange witnesses to incidents. I just hope that it helps vindicate me, and does not put the witnesses into the position of not being believed.

After more than thirty years of working in theater, I have, somehow, shifted into the film world. In theater, I, usually, found myself typecast as a fairy, sprite, mermaid, fairy godmother or some other such mythical, magical, GOOD creature. On the wrong side of fifty, sixty even, I have been telling them that I am getting on for skipping around the stage waving wands and suchlike. It just happens to be true that, it is the baddy characters which are so much more fun to play and get your teeth into, despite the adage that there are no small parts, just small actors.

It is incredibly stress relieving to let yourself go, playing someone nasty, especially in Zimbabwe, where we have an unbelievable amount of stress. (I received a poster on social media the other day which said, "Living in Zimbabwe should be added in your CV, it's a skill." For us it is a very amusing thing to say, because it is completely true. Luckily, we are very skilled at "making a plan" and helping each other out.)

My first scene as a terrorist (it might not be suitable for my age either, but it is definitely fun) I kicked the chair our victim was tied to, and it crashed to the floor, taking the helpless actor with it. Fortunately, he was uninjured and took it in good part. It felt GOOOOOD!

Our present film project involves scenes in a game park. The process for getting permission is arduous and time consuming, and involves visits to many government offices, and letter exchanging and phone calls. Anyway, Mr Spielberg (a very talented young African film maker, I am longing to see recognised) and I were sitting in a National Parks office – waiting – something, as an ADHD character, I am not good at. Looking for something to occupy my mind, I spotted a picture of a bird. Something about the shape of the bird was familiar, but I could not place it. I asked both the ladies in the office what kind of bird it was, but they could not help me.

When Mr Spielberg and I arrived outside our gate, sitting on the wall, I spotted the exact same bird I had seen in the picture. In trepidation, I asked if Mr Spielberg could see what I saw, and exactly what it was he saw. To my relief, he did see what I saw. The bird turned out to be a species of kingfisher. I knew two species (pied and malachite), but had never come across a brown hooded kingfisher before. The beak must have been what had caught my attention. A kingfisher had no reason to be sitting on our wall – there is no water containing fish near us. Finding one sitting on my wall, when I had just been trying to identify its picture, was a bizarre coincidence.

The next incident, to be witnessed, happened when I was driving one of the teachers home.

As we pulled up at a robot, a very inebriated street person came up to my window. I handed him a packet of *maputi* from the pack I keep for people who ask for things on the street.

He looked at the packet, and I was thinking that he was displeased that it was not money. One of the reasons I carry food is that cash is quite difficult to come by. I do not always have time to stay one or two hours in the bank to draw $100 (usually in coins – often in 10c or 20c or 25c coins). At school, we have got into the habit of wrapping them in $1 amounts with sticky tape, for easier handling. One advantage of carrying around a heavy bag of coins is that you could use it to give any prospective thieves a hefty whack with your pocketbook. Sorry, I digress again.

Anyway, after a few seconds of contemplation, the street person took out two bank cards. Then it was Cassie and I who looked puzzled. We gazed at the man. He smiled and dropped two bank cards onto the dashboard. Cassie and I looked at each other. The man smiled and waved, the robot changed and we went on our way.

Cassie, who has a delightful and unique way of looking at things, suggested that he might have been making an attempt to pay for the *maputi*.

The general reaction to the story was that it was something that would only happen to me. However, this time it happened to Cassie too.

Oh God

I had been having a lot of pain from a trapped nerve in my back. Every morning I was waking up feeling like I was being attacked by a donkey on my butt and calf. By twisting about and doing contortions, I could usually release it after a couple of hours.

One particular morning, it was getting on for three hours, and I was still in agony. I was getting cranky and calling out bitterly to God in fervent prayer that it was enough, and pleading that He do something.

I had been sitting on the side of my bed, and my cell phone was on charge on the dressing table in front of me. I stood up, and the charger cable slipped between my toes, the phone described an arc through the air, and swooped beneath the bed.

I was twisting this way and that, standing on one leg with the other stuck in the air, trying to reach the phone without pinching the nerve. All to no avail, because the donkey bit me hard just as I got hold of the cord where it was attached to the phone.

"Oh, God!" I pleaded. "PLEASE, do something!"

From beneath the bed, came an American lady's voice. "Let me tell you about oh God. There was this person and God appeared to him as an old man . . ."

At this point, I had the phone dangling from its cord in front of my face, and it stopped talking. I laughed so much, that I imagine it was like a friend once described having gas at the dentist – "You can still feel the pain, but you do not care." Shortly afterwards, the pain was gone, and it has never been quite as bad since.

People told me that there was a Google app which can talk to you. I have never used Google on my phone, and when I checked to see if the app was on my phone, I found that - first the phone had to be switched on, then, swiped across, then Google had to be looked for on the next page, then it asked for a setting. I did not look further.

Some weeks later, I had a confirmation that it was not something ordinary. I was telling someone the story, and my phone was in my purse.

When I got back home, I went to check my messages. I switched on, swiped across, and there was a page open. It was headed *Oh God*, and was followed by a list of names. I recognised the names of Nelson Chamisa and Grace Mugabe, but none of the others.

It Seems to Be Catching

After Louis and May had been with us a few years, they began to have incidents of their own.

I have an amazing, eccentric friend called, Denise. She is passionate about many things and incredibly active in many areas. She has a heart of gold but a short fuse. She is about five feet tall, rotund and given to risqué jokes. One of her particular interests is in animals. At the time of her incident with my father and May, she was in her sixties.

My son, who was, and still is, an electronics and computer enthusiast (I thought it ironic when my husband bought him his first computer while on a visit to Japan that the instruction book started off, "This computer is not only for beginners but also for maniacs.") had recently installed an electric gate. When people rang the bell and you ascertained who they were by communicating through the intercom, you could press a button and the gate would open. The button had to be held down for about two seconds to engage.

At that time we had two large dogs, Jessie, a Border collie and Max, a dog of mixed breed (probably incorporating Rhodesian ridgeback and Great Dane) with unusually long legs, and a habit of nipping the butt of anyone who ran in his presence.

As I walked into the house one day, I could tell that something had happened to disturb the equilibrium of Louis and May's day. They were bristling.

When I asked what had happened, they poured out the story, taking it in turns to tell the bits which had affected them most. What I pieced together was that Denise had rung the bell and Louis was in the bathroom. May, almost blind and in a wheel chair was not able to get to the intercom or the gate button, so she summoned Spiwe, the domestic worker. Spiwe ascertained that Denise was at the gate and wished to be admitted. May told Spiwe to hold the button down; so she did.

The gate started to open, then closed, then opened, then closed. . . Denise was shouting a commentary down the intercom. Max had taken the opportunity to go out of the gate to mark some territory.

Eventually, Spiwe took her finger off the button and the gate closed, trapping Max as he was making his way back inside, having satisfactorily made his communications on the outside.

Denise became besides herself.

More by luck than design, Spiwe finally succeeded in releasing Max and admitting Denise.

Denise fuming, charged into the house and let lose a stream of abuse at May and Louis (who had just entered the room and had been unaware of the goings on with the gate). The politest thing she had said was that they were not fit to be left in charge of an electric gate.

"She did not even say, hello," finished Louis indignantly.

The next time I entered the house into an atmosphere, there was a bit of a family gathering, Louis, May and my stepsister were all sitting in the lounge with the air of people in a doctor's waiting room. I looked quizzically at them. My impression was confirmed by May's first words, which, by the way, did not include a greeting.

"Your father thinks his testicles have turned black and we are waiting for Ted to come and look at them."

Unable to think of a single thing to say, I went into the kitchen for a glass of water.

Fortunately, it was a false alarm.

Appendix

Meeting May – *Koeksisters – a type of doughnut dipped in syrup, presented in a plait shape - an Africaans recipe*

A Real Thai Letter - *IAMWALKININARESTARONGTHREEDA ISATNITFROMSEVTOTWEL – I am working in a restaurant three days at night from seven to twelve*

Changing a light bulb - *Budza – a type of hoe*

See I Am Not Making Them up – *Maputi – a type of popcorn made with large cornels*

The Day I Thought the World Had Come to an End – *SPCA – Society for the Prevention of Cruelty to animals*

See, I Am Not Making Them Up – *Nelson Chamisa – Opposition Leader in Zimbabwe (MDC-T)*

See, I Am Not Making Them Up – *Grace Mugabe – Wife of Robert Gabriel Mugabe (Zimbabwe President for 38 years)*

About the author

Rebecca Viljoen was born in Bulawayo, Zimbabwe in 1953. She lives with her husband, and they have two grown up sons - who do not live with them. (They live with three cats and a flock of mixed breed bantam-type chickens.) Home is Harare, Zimbabwe. She has always lived in Africa, where her heart is, though she has travelled to most of the other continents. Her training is in special needs teaching for dyslexic and ADD/ADHD students, and she is the founder of a small educational trust, which specialises in students who do not fit comfortably into the ordinary school system. A few years ago, she met two young men in a car park, which somehow lead to her becoming a film producer. Although she knew nothing about film making, thirty years of experience in theater helped a little. Rebecca Viljoen is a *nom de plume*.

About the Illustrator

Bill Masuku is a born and raised Zimbabwean comic book artist, writer, and founder of Enigma Comix Africa. He gained acclaim for his fresh take on super hero narratives in his books *Captain South Africa* and *Razor-Man*, fast making him one of the notable pioneers of African comic book stories in the SADC region. He appeared as a guest at the first Comic Con Africa hosted in Johannesburg, South Africa in 2018. He has gone on to teach his craft in youth development programs in Harare.

Printed in the United States
By Bookmasters